ANOTHER FINE BOOK FOR MARRIED LOVERS
by Fr. Chuck Gallagher, S.J.

Fr. Chuck Gallagher, S.J., is a leading figure largely responsible for the dynamic development of the Marriage Encounter movement in the United States. Father Gallagher's unique ability to communicate the challenge of love and commitment has enhanced the experience of thousands of married couples nationwide.

His *Love Is a Couple* provides compelling insights into achieving an open, creative, and fulfilling love relationship. As love evolves, the depth of discovery calls for realizing and dealing with shared responsibility, changing needs, and mutual trust.

His *Parents Are Lovers* focuses on the broader relationship of married couples that expands with children and portrays the challenge of parenting, which can lead to further enrichment and invigorating love. The book instills the means to attain togetherness, warmth, and love in the context of a family.

LOVE TAKES GREATNESS, the latest addition to his marriage series, is a book for *all* married lovers—young and old—who cherish their commitment in love and strive for even greater sharing and caring within the marriage relationship.

LOVE TAKES
GREATNESS

LOVE TAKES GREATNESS

Complete and Unabridged

Fr. Chuck Gallagher, S.J.

edited and arranged by Bob and Lois Blewett

IMAGE BOOKS
A DIVISION OF DOUBLEDAY & COMPANY, INC.
GARDEN CITY, NEW YORK
1980

Image Book edition published September,
1980 by special arrangement with
William H. Sadlier, Inc.

Library of Congress Catalog
Card Number: 79–6884
ISBN: 0-385-15972-2
Printed in the United States of America

Dear Lovers—

Here is an unfinished book. It is yet to be completed by you. More important than what I have written will be what *you* write! Please take the time—and love—to jot beside the opening photos your own private, special wishes. And as you read the book, answer the questions and talk about them with each other. The purpose of the book is to bring you closer together. That's the best thing you can do to make your marriage great!

Happy writing (and reading).

Enjoy,

Chuck

Fr. Chuck Gallagher

Our love is great—now. May it be forever.

I WISH FOR US . . .

That we keep the magic of the day we met.

. . . and never lose our first love.

That we always uphold each other as we did at the beginning.

am
(I ~~was~~ so proud of you!)

that we are always alive to each other.
            together with friends . . .

or alone with our letters.

Shared hurts—

ecstatic love—

perpetual oneness.

that we continue to grow together . . .

as we share our triumphs . . .

and our problems—face-to-face.

That we keep on seeing the good in each other.

And keep on planning our next big adventure!

MY WISHES FOR "US."
(THE THINGS ABOUT YOU—
ABOUT US—THAT I WANT TO
LAST FOREVER.)

HUSBAND'S   WIFE'S
WISHES   WISHES

TO BE MORE THAN MARRIED SINGLES, WE NEED TO TAKE ON EACH OTHER'S VALUES AND FIND "COUPLE" GOALS.

1

VALUES

What are values?   *Your answer:*

Everyone has values. Probably no two people have the same values in the same order of importance, but they have them. It is our values which determine the direction of our lives.

There is usually a positive quality about them. Trust means a great deal to us. Beauty, truth, goodness are important. So is sincerity. And loyalty and fidelity. Integrity, sociability, spirituality, security, education, popularity. Godliness, patriotism, family ties, religion—the list is endless.

The values we have are our basic motives for doing what we do. They provide the purpose and direction of our lives. The summation of our values is the vision we have of what our lives are all about.

There are occasions when two good values can lead to conflicting choices. The value of generosity, for example, could be in opposition to the value of security. Or the value of family ties could be in opposition to concern for our neighbors.

Not all values are practical, lived-out experiences in each

of our lives. It isn't that any one of them is not good. But some values are more important to us than others. It's probably difficult for us to even recognize what values we actually have and terribly hard to rank them.

The only way we can discover what our values really are is to look at the decisions we make and the way we live. For example, we may say that religious values mean the most to us, especially when it comes to bringing up our children. Yet we may live in a neighborhood of diverse values where there is little possibility that such a value can be imbedded in our children's hearts. Or we may say that close family ties are our overriding value, yet we never seem to get around to having much time for one another.

A teacher might say, for example, that his highest value in life is his relationship with his pupils, but has no time for conversation with them, even in the classroom. He spends most of his time reading. His search for truth is a higher value. In other words, if we want to find out what our values are, we need to look at the way we're living and examine the direction in which our major decisions lead. It's also important to know which values have our priority on an overall basis as well as in specific circumstances. Sometimes they vary.

Disillusionment is prevalent when it comes to discerning our values. We know we're decent, good people, and we think our values are good, reasonable, and set for life. We think we've decided the way we want to live and that we're doing it. But we may rearrange our values at various turning points in our lives. If we were asked at age 16 what our values are, and then at 26, and again at 56, we are apt to discover some differences, and yet each time we would be sincere.

We can probe to find out what we value most highly now. For a beautiful, sound husband-and-wife relationship, it is essential that we share with each other, our values, the basis for our ambitions and goals.

Why did you marry each other?   *Your answer:*

When hearts beat faster and bells ring and we find each other physically attractive, a natural chemistry is in operation. An appealing face and figure is one of the first factors in getting us to look at each other as possible mates.

Later we're inclined to put less emphasis on this motivation because we lose some of our physical attractiveness through the years. Furthermore, we recognize that physical attractiveness in itself is not enough to hold a marriage together even though the impact may have been powerful at first.

In our dating days there were a number of people we met who turned us on with their good looks. We were very much aware of these individuals, yet we didn't go out with them, or if we did, we dropped them after a short period of time. Why? In the simplest terms it was because we found they were not "our kind of person." While they may have looked great, they didn't have the personality to keep us turned on. We might have said things like, "Wow, what a great figure, but above the neck she's dead." Or, "I get butterflies in my stomach when I look at him, but he's so self-centered." Or, "She's pretty, but she just chatters on and on about nothing." Or, "He's handsome, but so dull." Even in the earlier stages of dating we were looking for more than physical attractiveness. We were looking for qualities we could relate to, admire and appreciate.

What we were looking for was someone with whom we could be open, someone who was warm and receptive so that we could relax and be ourselves. Although we may not have used the word "compatibility," that's what we were searching for. Instinctively we realized that being in relationship went far beyond being physically attracted.

To be able to say, "He understands me," or, "She listens to

me," was important. We were looking for someone with whom we could communicate, to whom we could talk. We were interested in learning everything about the other person, and we wanted the other person to know us. There were many things that we wouldn't talk about to anyone else. We were looking for someone with whom we could share the secrets of our heart.

I know a couple who appeared to be as different as night and day. Vi was a fun girl, the lively one at any party. She was off on trips and vacations as often as she could take them. She was up on the latest styles and was always seen at the newest place. Tad was the quiet and reserved type. When he did go to a party, he was gawky. She was a spritely sunbeam, full of personality and excitement, always on the go. He was like an oak. He was there, but not noticed. Most people thought there wasn't much to him.

Vi told me that they'd lived on the same block all their lives and she had always thought Tad was one of those grey, sad people. There didn't seem to be any fun in his life. Tad told me that he had thought Vi was a surface kind of person, with sparkle, but nobody to think twice about. During the blackout in New York they were stuck together in an elevator for three hours. He found out that she believed in all the things he did. That she wanted out of life exactly what he wanted out of life. And she found out that he was really her kind of guy.

He had always found himself tongue-tied with girls. But there in the elevator he sensed an empathy between them and he talked freely. The more he talked the more she seemed to understand. They were so absorbed in each other that they forgot the stalled elevator and the discomfort of sitting scrunched in a corner. Each was excited to find how much alike they were. It almost became a game of "stump me" as they both poured out what they looked for in life, bringing out from the core of themselves what they had carefully hidden.

The time in that elevator was like life in the catacombs in pagan Rome where the early Christians could safely talk. Family ties were precious to them. They both believed that it was more important to have a few real friends than to know a lot of people casually. God and the Church were essential to the well-being of each of them; they both loved and wanted children but they were determined not to have their home revolve around the kids; books were more interesting than school; neither of them were terribly excited about careers and getting ahead; they both considered gentleness very manly and neither of them thought that a woman had to give up tenderness to be modern; both of them wanted to find happiness in the quality of their marriages. With them, when the lights went out, the lights came on! And they've stayed on.

When we were dating and you told me you loved roughing it, I didn't dream you meant canoeing, too!

What holds you together as a couple?

Your answer:

There are many things that keep couples together. Most obviously, our children and the fact that we're married. We develop a certain lifestyle together, each of us important to the other in it. Furthermore we have a shared history that binds us together. We've faced crises together and helped each other through. We've experienced joys and a tremendous amount of love.

But what most binds us together are the *values* we share. This is the glue that keeps us together. It is the foundation of our relationship. Values are the things that make our life worthwhile. They are at the root of our decisions and they give us integrity and worth as persons. They encompass the dreams and the ambitions that are dear to our hearts. It is in our values that we have more security of consistency than in anything else.

Everything else between us is on a day-to-day changing basis. Feelings vary—sometimes from minute to minute. Our relationship with our children changes continually. We may change our domiciles, our standard of living. Friends may come and go. Our relationships with our family can be drastically affected by death or separation or human failing. There is little in a relationship that can be considered stable, only our values.

In our love relationship, *feelings* give it "go" power. That's what turns us on to each other, puts the sparkle in our eyes and the smile on our lips. But feelings come and go. *Values* give it "stay" power. The beauty of what is stable and exclusive in the marital relationship comes out of a value commitment. Consequently, our values are at the core of our love for each other. They determine the depth and strength and beauty and goodness of our love and our responsiveness to

32

each other. Values are the spine, the skeleton, upon which we place the flesh-and-blood of our feelings.

It is most important in a marital relationship for a husband and wife to see each other's goodness. That goodness is discerned in the things they hold dear, the values they deem important. The deep personhood of a man or a woman is best defined by his or her values. Even at times when a husband doesn't seem very attractive, his values are always there and he is attractive in them!

The more conscious we become of each other's values, the more closely knit we will become as a couple. When we lose sight of our values or assume the other person is going in another direction, there is unhappiness and misunderstanding.

My friend Tom was very dissatisfied with himself at one time. He wasn't providing the life for his wife, Terry, that he felt she deserved. Money was usually tight and he was frequently upset because his work was such a strain. He didn't see himself as much of a success at marriage, and yet, he had had so many dreams when they walked down the aisle!

Terry was equally worried. She knew that Tom saw himself as a failure with her. When they were first married she looked forward to having more money than they turned out to have, but she was very satisfied with their marriage. Sure, there were things she didn't have. But she had a basic confidence in Tom and in herself. She wished he did.

Then something happened to change things. An evening last fall started out with a pleasant surprise. The kids went off to bed without a lot of bother and fell asleep as soon as they were under the covers. Tom and Terry relaxed together. They began to talk. At first Tom was apologetic. "Honey, I haven't given you the house we wanted and our furniture is something we'd have to persuade the Salvation Army to take. It's a squeeze to take you out even twice a month, and you have to watch every penny when you go to the store. Why, you can only call your mother a few times a year because we can't afford the bills. We have nothing put away. What kind of life is this for you?"

"It's good," said Terry, "I see that a couple can be happy even if they don't have everything they thought they wanted.

I have what I want—a life where the two of us and the children are more important than anything else. We're kind to each other and we appreciate it that our friends are kind. We're both more ambitious for this to be a better world than we are to get ahead. We enjoy doing things for other people. Sure, I can't call Mom very often, but she knows she's thought of fondly by both of us."

Tom started putting two and two together, "My mother gets more attention from you than she gets from my sisters. Every mother-in-law should be so lucky! And you put us— you and me—first, even before the children! Everyone in the neighborhood trusts you, and neither of us are complainers. We not only make do—we have a great time together. I still wish I was going to make more money, but I wouldn't trade for what we've got."

Harmonizing together at the piano means a lot to both of us.

Terry summed up their realizations. "We are good for each other. I usually think of myself as the one who doesn't make good choices, but I couldn't have done better where it really counts. I chose you, and I would do it again." Those words put Tom back on the high road.

Values change little from year to year. They are very likely the same as those we had when we first met. We may express them differently or we may have an increased or decreased opportunity to exercise them, but the basic values remain the same. It was these values that made "him" my kind of guy, that revealed "her" as my type of gal.

Since our values had been pretty much determined by the time we were married, and they will be modified only slightly during our lives, they are the most secure foundation on which to rest our relationship. We're not going to wake up some day to find our beloved a stranger with a completely different value system.

We should recognize that those values in which we see alike are a gift of our love for each other. They are a part of our "coupleness" and our security for the future.

What would you ask for if you had three wishes?

1.

2.

3.

The fairy godmother is a traditional figure in children's literature. But fairy tales appeal to adults as well. The notion of having three wishes granted is very attractive. We know it's a dream, but it's such a nice dream! It would be so wonderful if it could be true!

Part of such fairy tales is that the people who are granted their three wishes make foolish choices. We are certain that if we were ever granted that opportunity we would never be so silly. Our choices would be wise ones. We long for the chance to prove it.

All right. Imagine that your fairy godmother is tapping your shoulder with her magic wand. She is going to grant you three wishes. What will they be?

If there is a serious health problem in the family, that would certainly be number one on your list.

And in all probability one of your wishes would have something to do with money. It isn't that you would want a tremendous amount of money, but you'd like to have a little bit more than you have now. And you'd like a little bit nicer home or a better school to which to send your children. And maybe a job for your husband in which he could be happier. Your wishes might include a special place to visit, or personal qualities you'd like to have, such as peace of mind, or for the family, harmony.

It could be that your horizons are very broad; you might ask for peace on earth, a decent standard of living for everyone everywhere, and the opportunity for all people to be free. You might wish that everybody would have somebody to understand him, that gentleness and kindness would rule on the face of the earth, and that all children would be truly loved and cared for.

Oh, there are so many wishes that all of us could think of! There are too many from which to choose. The decision-making gets really hard when it comes down to the third wish. Maybe the first two regarding health and money are pretty obvious, but when we know that we have only one wish left, it's terrible. So we might try to cheat a little and wish that we have all the wishes we want!

What do your wishes say about your values?

The wishes that we decide on indicate where our hearts are.

If we were asked what we value most highly, we would probably name high-minded values—not necessarily to impress people—but because we honestly think we act according to them. It's only when we get down to the nitty-gritty of choosing what we want for ourselves—for the actual situations we are in—that it's a different story.

It isn't that we don't hold humanistic values, it's just that they don't affect our daily living. And much of the time we're not aware of the values on which we base our everyday decisions! It is important for us to figure out what our values are, so that we can see how they are affecting the way we live with each other as husband and wife.

Here are some questions to ask ourselves. How many of our wishes are self-centered? (We can look, too, at the ten or twelve wishes we wanted but had to discard.) In deciding if a wish is self-centered, we have to be honest. A wife may wish for a better job for her husband, but she's actually thinking of how the increase in salary would make things better for herself. A husband may wish for a promotion or a raise, thinking it is important to him in terms of what it will do for his wife and the kids, but deep down inside he wants it because it will make him feel better as a provider.

How many of our choices are "thing"-centered? A bigger home? More conveniences? A new car? We're not trying to be naive here and suggest that money is not important. Of course it is, and it has an impact on our life. To live in poverty is nobody's ideal. But how large does money loom in our thinking?

37

A big question to ask ourselves is, "If it were not the fairy godmother but God who appeared to us and said, 'Ask of me anything you want,' what would our list have been?" Most of us, if we're honest, would have to admit that it would be different, because if it were God, we would be thinking in spiritual terms, which implies that we consider the spiritual aspects of our life to be something separate from normal everyday living. That gives us quite a subject to ponder, doesn't it?

How many of our wishes are in regard to our marriage? It's fairly safe to claim that all of us think marriage is the most precious experience of our lives, but is it possible that not one wish of the three concerned our marriage? If so, that would indicate that our marriage isn't one of our more pressing concerns. We could say to ourselves that we're doing all right, but right now we need more money—the children have needs and the house is falling apart. The question that was asked, however, was what three wishes you want granted, not what three problems you want solved or what three barriers you are facing.

The omission of marriage from the list speaks volumes, doesn't it? It says that our ambitions for our marriage are pretty well satisfied, that we aren't looking for anything more! Are we saying that we don't see any way our relationship could be better or that other things have greater significance for us? If someone said that money was the most important thing and then didn't have money on his list of wishes, we would think him rather inconsistent. If another person claimed that religion was the most significant value in his life, yet it didn't appear among his wishes, we'd question his sincerity.

So if we say that our marriage is what makes our life worthwhile, and then we make three wishes with not one focusing in on marriage, we may well question what we meant. It isn't that we're dishonest; it's just that our values aren't what we think they are.

If marriage *did* come up on our list of wishes, what was its thrust? Did the wish center on some dissatisfaction or irritant. Perhaps we are misunderstood, our spouse is drinking too much or is too absorbed in the children. And we want life to

38

I'm glad we think alike about words—but more important is "us." Let's always be special to each other.

be more comfortable. No one is trying to say that the wish is not legitimate. But it is focused more on taking away something than on adding something. Furthermore, it hinges on the other person's changing.

Possibly we have a wish centered on just having a good marriage. That seems to be a good and positive wish, and it is focused in on the relationship. But what we mean by a "good marriage" must be examined. That, too, could be a general way of asking that the other person change. What we are implying is that if the other person listened to us more or talked to us more or participated more in our activities, our marriage would be better.

Because our wishes reveal our values, we need to reassess them. Then we can work on them alone and with our spouse in order to have the values that we sincerely want. We can discover what is behind some of our frustrations and our lack of understanding, and we can try to see how we need to upgrade the value of marriage in our daily consciousness.

How often do you talk about each other's values?

Your answer:

Just as it's important for us to discover our individual values and not assume that we know what they are, we must discover our spouses' values—we don't automatically know what they are.

We may hold something to be so important that we can't conceive of our spouse having anything other than that same value. A husband might see supporting his family as being of the utmost seriousness in his life. His every thinking moment is centered around doing his job well. He can't imagine anything having greater importance than that, and he assumes that his wife feels the same way. He takes for granted that she understands why he makes certain decisions about the amount of time away from home and the degree of physical and emotional energy he's pouring into his occupation. It never enters his mind that she might consider something else to be of greater importance. But she may see as a higher value, his being at home—not just being present in the house, but having some energy left to give to her and the children. She rates the things he provides as less important.

Also, she might have an absolute conviction that it's important for her not to stagnate as a person. This reality is so clear in her mind that she assumes that any thinking person would agree. She feels her husband's priorities are the same as hers and that he will make all sorts of sacrifices. But he doesn't feel that way. When he hears her speak of participating in community affairs or getting a job for self-fulfillment, he hears the words but doesn't take them seriously. He simply can't believe that such a thing is her number one priority.

Obviously there are going to be serious misunderstandings between the couple. It is not that one is right and the other wrong, but they don't know and understand each other's values.

Sometimes one person does have a good idea of what the other's values are, but his own values are so strong and clear for him that he has no intention of adapting them to his spouse. What takes place then is not communication but an announcement, and it is without maliciousness or evil intent. The person says, "This is the way I am and this is the way I'm going to be."

When we get caught in such a situation, it's because we're so set in our values that we take it for granted that they are completely obvious. We assume that the other person must have the same values. If you are not seeing with my eyes, I may feel, "That's tough—you're going to have to learn to live with my values just as I have to learn to live with yours."

What we're actually doing is placing other values above that of our relationship. We are making our relationship sub-

41

ject to other things. Rather, we should see that our most important value in life is a deep relationship with our beloved.

When we adjust our perspective, our highest ambition will be to love each other, be aware of each other, understand each other, be responsive to each other. We will subject all other values to that of our relationship.

How much do you appreciate each other's values?

Your answer:

In a good husband-and-wife relationship, there has to be a deep appreciation for each other. The better the relationship, the more total the appreciation.

When I try to fit your values into mine instead of accepting the fact that you have values that are meaningful to you, it doesn't help our relationship.

We need to be open to each other's thinking, not just for the purpose of considering the other's values to see whether or not they hurt our lifestyle, but to recognize our partner's right to his own values and our privilege to get involved in them. Few people appreciate the husband who considers the money he earns to be all his—even if he is generous and gives his wife everything she asks for. Nor do people applaud the wife who looks on the children as "hers."

We can appreciate our beloved's values only when we try to taste and experience his principles and ambitions the way he does. We have to approach the other person's values not in order to evaluate them objectively to see whether or not we like them, but in order to feel them in the same way as our spouse does.

We are not to give up our individual values. It's not a question of subtracting—but of adding! We need to accept the other person's values, looking on them as precious and real.

I know of a family in which incidents of tension kept cropping up with the kids whenever the parents took them any place or when people visited. Charlie liked the kids to have good manners and be nicely dressed when they went out. Yvonne thought Charlie was a bit of a stuffed shirt. Charlie agreed that he was, but he figured that, after all, the kids had to learn manners someplace.

One day Charlie asked Yvonne, "What makes you act as though you don't care how our kids dress or act? I know you don't want them to grow up barbarians." Yvonne explained that she didn't want to do with their kids what families in her generation had done. She wanted their children to exhibit

Hey, Grampa. Guess who wants to go fishing?

43

manners as a courtesy to others rather than as a regiment of do's and don'ts. She knew too many people who were perfectly proper but weren't at all considerate of people. Talking it out helped a great deal. They recognized they still had to face the problem of carrying one or the other view too far, but then they understood each other. Charlie agreed with Yvonne's value wholeheartedly and she did with his.

It isn't that a couple should give a blank check to each other's principles or switch their opinions so they can agree with each other's position or that each should adopt the other's stand contrary to his own. Rather, it is to get behind the principles, the position, the stand, and experience the value that is being held. A principle, a position or a stand can be wrong, sometimes even bad, but a value is never wrong. It's always good. It may not be as good as the person makes it out to be, but a value is good. Financial security may not be as important as the preservation of life, but it is a positive value. Being liked by the neighbors can lead us to excesses and compromise, but it's good in itself.

Because we're human we can get carried away and give a disproportionate amount of importance to one value or another. Or we might have one value loom so large in our consciousness that we exclude all others. Nonetheless, a value is a value. It is good in itself. Consequently when our husband or wife has a different value than we have, it isn't a choice between good and bad, it's a choice between *good* and *good*.

It's important for us, therefore, to experience the good that our spouse sees in that value. Otherwise we're just dealing objectively with his value. We're standing outside and analyzing it. In a couple relationship we're supposed to take on each other, share with each other. When you offer me your value, I can't just say I don't want yours, I have a better one. Yours is important to you and worthwhile. I have to see what you find so good about it! I need to understand what makes it so vital to your life.

This value may have been ingrained in you by your upbringing. You may have grown up in poverty, so the memory of wearing hand-me-downs and being dependent upon others for food and shelter is painful. Naturally, the value of financial independence is going to be big to you. The decisions we make about money should not be totally conditioned by the experience of one or the other of us, but we should have an appreciation of each other's values concerning money so that we can have a better understanding of each other.

It could be that one of us grew up in a home where the way of life was so different from that of the neighbors that we were isolated and rejected. Because of those circumstances we may have a tremendous desire to get along with our present neighbors. We don't want the same thing to happen to our children that happened to us. Our spouse needs to know that.

Experiences should not be used as excuses to act against higher principles and more pressing values. Instead they should develop our understanding and our ability to appreciate the other person.

This is part of the real empathy that we must have for each other, so that we will be able to walk in our beloved's shoes.

What problems do you encounter because of different values?   *Your answer:*

Because we approach decisions in certain areas from different perspectives it will be at times that one of us is saying black and the other is saying white. Our values are in conflict and we experience frustration. When we have the same values, we're in harmony. They may not be values that anybody else agrees with, but if we two agree on them they are a bond between us. We are pointing in the same direction. We experience a sense of unity, a common focus in life. When we have different values in any area—the home, the children, money or the church—we experience discord. There is a breach. We find it difficult to sympathize with each other.

For example, a husband—let's call him Tony—wants the children to be prepared to get ahead in this world, to make a decent living. His wife, Sylvia, is more concerned that the children be happy. It isn't that Tony doesn't want the children to be happy, but he assumes that the only way they're ever going to be happy is if they have decent jobs. It's very difficult for him to understand how anybody could be happy if he were always scratching around, not knowing where the next meal was coming from. On the other hand, Sylvia is more concerned with the present. Both have good values, but there will be a conflict whenever they make decisions about the children's education, discipline, special lessons.

Another case: Harold might put a tremendous value on making sure that Jane and the children are provided for in case death or sickness comes to him. It is in the forefront of his consciousness. Whenever a decision has to be made in an area of finances, he is strongly motivated to keep a tight control on the budget. He wants to save. He wants to be in-

You've shown me another dimension.

volved in pension plans. He has a vision of his wife and children being destitute and being on welfare or at the mercy of neighbors or family charity. His fears are reinforced by stories about family men struck down in their prime. On the other hand, Jane is facing immediate needs. She doesn't have the same urgency for saving as Harold has. To her it's far more important that they live a full life together now than that she have plenty of money when he is gone. She sees his goal as reducing their present standard of living.

Obviously there are all sorts of built-in conflicts connected with those two values. Harold and Jane each need to look at the values of the other, recognizing the decision that each is inclined to make and how that interferes with the carrying out of each other's values. If they don't, any time money comes up there will be a battle. They may work out compromises, but that's not furthering their relationship. It's far more important to get to the root of the problem and strengthen their coupleness.

By each of them taking on the values of the other person their decisions will be modified. In decisions regarding money they will each have a much deeper understanding of the step the other proposes. They will be much more at ease making a joint new decision than they would have been with either of the ones they were first inclined to make. Too, neither is going to experience surrender. The couple will have a taste of the value behind the common decision they make. Jane will find it easier to make the sacrifices that are necessary for putting aside money. Harold won't feel betrayed because she wants to enjoy an occasional evening out with him.

There is another problem in holding separate goals. It emphasizes our individuality. It is true that each of us is a unique person, but husband and wife are expected to share, not only their material goods, but also their personhoods. The sharing can't be on the physical level only; it needs to include the spiritual, a sharing of the body and the soul. One of the most beautiful things about a husband and wife is the values they prize. This is what most identifies their coupleness. It would be a pity if a man and woman lived together in marriage and did not share their values. Worse than the conflicts and the power struggle that so often develop in those circumstances, there is goodness that is being missed. What if a husband is a great poet and his wife doesn't appreciate poetry? What if a wife has a great talent for art and her husband has no interest in it? Our values are important and wonderful, and if the person who's dearest to us doesn't appreciate them, we feel half destroyed.

Is there a difference between values held by a husband and wife individually and "couple" values?

Your answer:

A couple is a perfect example of the whole being greater than the sum of its parts. Sometimes we think that a couple brings their individual talents, education, and other qualities into a marriage and then each one has a little bit more than he started with. They make up for each other's deficiencies; he's strong in the area where she's weak, and vice versa. They count on each other. That's not what marriage is. That's a partnership. Somebody who has money but not much talent gets together with somebody who has talent but not much money, and they're both happy. Or somebody who's a good salesman gets together with somebody who has a good product and they reinforce each other.

Marriage is not a partnership, it is a *union!* Each gives the fullness of who he is.

In thinking that the husband has his life and the wife has hers and the two of them together get along very well, we have a roommate type of situation, not a marriage. They are just married singles!

In too many cases, a husband has his way of doing things and a wife has her way and both do their own thing as long as they don't interfere with each other. It seems easy. There is less friction and fewer conflicts. That is true, but there's also less unity. If we want to be united, we need to work at our oneness.

It is not simply a question of accommodating each other's habits or idiosyncrasies, it goes much deeper. We look at an older couple and are struck by how much they look alike. Seeing their wedding pictures we'd never guess that they could ever resemble each other because their faces looked so different. What has happened is that they've taken on each other's smile lines and frown lines. If they've been a serious couple, that shows on their faces. If they've been a joyful couple, that also shows. It's not merely the shrinkage of old age that has brought about the physical similarity, it's their living together and being influenced by each other.

The exterior similarity has been created by the state of mind of the husband and wife over the years. Although muscles can't be controlled directly, they're affected by things we can control—basically, the decisions we make about the kind of couple we want to be. In the same way, an interior conformation can take place.

Our coupleness includes an assumption of each other's values. Nothing can lead to greater joy and fulfillment for a couple than for each to gradually begin to shape himself in accordance with the goals, ideals and visions of his beloved. It's a delight to know we have somebody who thinks as we do, someone whom we instinctively recognize will come up with the same approach as we have to things.

One of the beauties of human friendship, attested to in song and story, is that a friend is an alter ego. When my friend is present, I am present. We can speak for each other because we're tuned in to each other. We share common dreams and our lives have become integrated.

If this is true of friendship, how much more it can be true in a good marriage! However, if we leave it to chance, it may not happen. We have to make it happen. We have to become so much a confidant of each other, so open and responsive to each other, that this internal oneness can gradually, marvelously, take place.

We're more than "married singles."

I love you.

2

WHEN CRITICISM IS ABSENT,
ROMANCE HAS A CHANCE TO
ENTER OUR LIVES.

CRITICISM

What is criticism?   *Your answer:*

What in the world is criticism? If you add up a column of figures incorrectly or you say we're supposed to be Grandma's on Wednesday and she is expecting us on Thursday and I tell you so, that's correcting facts. That's not criticism. However, when I ascribe a negative motivation to your mistake I'm criticizing.

We're not always content with pointing out an inaccuracy. We go on and attribute it to a character defect. I not only say that you forgot the date we were planning to have—I have to add, "You never care about things that are important to me!" Maybe you didn't iron my shirt or fix my socks, so I call you a "Women's Libber." It's one thing to remind you that my Uncle Joe doesn't like to be called Joey; it's quite another thing to tell you that you call him Joey because you don't like my family. I should be able to say that I think one of your decisions is wrong without my adding that it's wrong because you lack common sense.

All of us accept the fact that we make mistakes, but when a mistake is blamed on a character defect or a personality failing, the comment is a personal attack and a put-down.

When we assume that a person's action means that he is deliberately doing something because we disapprove of it, or that he's doing it for any other negative reason, we are making the worst interpretation. And we are in the wrong.

We can disagree with each other's positions or decisions without criticizing. Disagreements happen even in a good husband-and-wife relationship. But we cannot assign negative qualities of character or personality to our spouse's position or decision without our comments becoming criticism. And, after all, our judgment could be wrong. In many cases, what we may consider a faulty stand has come out of the best intentions in the world, or from what is actually an admirable quality. A young woman I know is devoted to her mother. Sylvia's feelings are based on honest and sincere affection. It is not because of a little-girl mentality or a dependent personality. However, her caring has led her to make a mistake in judgment regarding the amount of time she should spend with her mother. Sylvia's husband is determined to give a fair day's work for a fair day's pay, and he deeply desires to get ahead for the sake of his family. This leads him to make a mistake in judgment regarding the amount of work he has to do to satisfy his boss.

Even if Sylvia gives too much time to her mother, and even if her husband has put an undue emphasis on his job, criticism is not the proper way to solve the problems. Criticism leads to hurt and drives us away from being open and honest in our communication with each other. It makes it difficult for us to be responsive. It can make us more determined than ever to assert our way of doing things and to insist that we're right. It prevents full-hearted and generous loving.

Criticism also breaks our spirit. It makes us lose appreciation of our own goodness and worth. It tears down any self-confidence that we have.

We believe that our spouse knows us better than anybody else, and we trust that he really loves us. So if he tells us something negative—that we're lazy or selfish or indifferent, that we don't have good judgment or a sense of humor—we accept it as part of our character and personality. That's probably the worst thing about criticism—it is accepted! We make it part of our own self-evaluation. We agree that our spouse is correct in his analysis of us. Of course we all have traces of defects, so if our spouse ascribes a certain type of conduct to us, we begin to see it in ourselves. A great philosopher once said, "I am what I think." In the case of criticism it gets to be, "I am what *you* think."

Being criticized creates within us an atmosphere of personal failure. We become very conscious of what we do wrong and sublimate our positive capabilities. When a team plays for a coach who is always harping at them, always pointing out their mistakes, they play cautious ball. They concentrate their attention on *not making mistakes* rather than on winning the game. They do not risk the big play. Instead of getting absorbed in the game and playing up to their ability, they are self-conscious. They think about every move,

You always make me feel like a million dollars— whether we're at home or out with friends.

with an eye on the bench to see what the coach thinks.

The same thing can happen in a husband-and-wife relationship. When we are always critical, the other person thinks: "Now what is she going to say?" "How is he going to take this?" It takes the spontaneity and the joy out of the relationship. We can't be our true selves. We may cut down the number of mistakes we make, but in our carefulness we become dull and plodding. Our definition of a good mate is in terms of what we don't do rather than of our potential. A husband says, "I'm giving her nothing to complain about." A wife says, "He has nothing to be upset about with me." How much better if a husband could say, "I don't do everything just right, but she knows I help her in order to have more time with her," and a wife could say, "I'm not perfect, but he knows I want to please him more than anything in the world!"

What do you criticize   *Your answer:*
about your spouse?

When we criticize the one we love, it usually has to do with an area we consider to be a weakness or a failing. It may concern a personality trait or some character quality we don't happen to like. That is no sign that it's wrong!

Interestingly enough, what we consider a weakness of our spouse may stem from his greatest virtue. For instance Maggie may be distrustful of Sam's decisions because she feels he lets his heart rule his head. But Sam is a kind and thoughtful person, which is one of the reasons Maggie married him. Sam considers Maggie to be unfeeling and too harsh in the way she deals with others. But Maggie is sure of herself and reliable, which are the very qualities that first attracted Sam to her.

58

We also criticize our beloved for the very defects we have! We do it because then we don't look so bad. We feel that even if we do the same things, the other person is worse. I say disgustedly, "You're more careless than I am when it comes to money," or, "You're more strict with the children than I am."

On the other hand, we may realize our own failings and look to our spouse to be what we aren't. A wife may criticize her husband for not reminding her of a certain appointment. She may say, "You know I can't remember those things. You're supposed to cover for me. Why didn't you?" A husband who has a quick temper may expect his wife to get him out of situations when he blows up. A wife may find it difficult to stand up for her rights and principles, so she looks to her husband to do that for her. When he doesn't, she criticizes.

Behind our criticism may even be a "get even" mentality. "You've criticized me, so now I feel perfectly free to criticize you. As a matter of fact, I feel an impulse to do so because I don't want to be on the taking end all the time. I want to even things off."

When we hear about critical persons, we probably feel detached—we don't feel that *we* are critical. But we may be thinking about style rather than substance, feeling that we're not harsh or nasty, that we are soft-spoken and use a kindly manner. But if we are making negative assumptions, we are still criticizing!

Because criticism is so prevalent in our society, we may indulge in it less than the average person and still do it a lot! We may seldom criticize our neighbors, our friends or even our business associates, and yet be very critical around the house. It seems to be easier for us to be understanding of others than of our beloved. This is true because of our constant exposure to each other. We have more opportunity to criticize. We are also more affected by each other's weaknesses. It's much easier for us to put up with the defects of people we don't see very often or who don't affect us as much.

There's something more than that, though. We expect our spouse to put up with our criticism. A fellow employee, a friend or a neighbor wouldn't stand for it. They'd ask, "What right do you have to criticize me?" On the other hand, in our homes we each assume the other has the right. We feel that the greater the level of intimacy, the more right we have to criticize each other. That's a sad commentary on the husband-and-wife relationship. Let's change it!

What causes you to criticize?   *Your answer:*

Criticism arises over all sorts of situations: our having been inconvenienced or put on the spot, our getting upset over something or feeling neglected or pressured. When Fred is in a rush to get to the train and finds the gas tank empty, he complains to Louise that she's selfish. Or Louise is embarrassed by the way Fred talks at parties, so she tells him in no uncertain terms that he's insensitive.

Another base for our criticism is our being disappointed in marriage. We have an image of what a husband or wife should be like. Being married, we see that our dream isn't all true. Instead of forgetting the dream and accepting the real person, we tend to give up the real person and keep fussing away, trying to match the other person to our expectations. Frequently a man wants his wife to cook as his mother did, or the way he thinks she did. Or, he remembers how she got him up in the mornings, how she always had his laundry neatly put away, how there was always a snack ready. He has all kinds of role expectations into which a woman is supposed to fit. When he finds out that his wife has other talents or that she has different goals for their relationship, he tends to believe he's been let down, that he's been cheated in his marriage. So he picks away at her, maybe not directly but subtly.

No criticizing. We're keeping this a love affair—as big as the whole state!

He is the nice guy putting up with his wife's deficiencies, but he very well lets her know about it.

A woman may know that her husband-to-be doesn't share all her dreams or even consider them to be particularly attractive, but she figures that after they're married he'll come around—for her. She'll get him to change. When she finds that he's sloppy around the house and doesn't pitch in and help her, that he expects her to keep everything spic and span by herself, that he doesn't always look on her conversation as scintillating, that he falls into the category of many husbands when it comes to watching sports or television or being absorbed in his job, she thinks she's perfectly justified in her right to complain. She believes that changes will be accomplished only if she lets him know how much he's failing her.

We also criticize when we want the other person to do or not do something. For instance, a wife, we'll call her Allison, tells her husband, Vic, how much it would mean to her to have him sit down and talk in the evening. She explains that she needs not only his economic support, but his spiritual support. For a couple of nights Vic relaxes and chats with her, but then he goes back to his same old pattern of working in the basement after supper. Allison starts picking at him, calling him a typical husband—married to his work, etc., etc. But what she is really saying is that she doesn't have any confidence that Vic loves her and will respond to her. She feels that instead of discussing it further, she has to try to force him to be different.

Every marriage starts with two people who have to learn to live together. They haven't had the experience of coupleness. Each is used to doing things his own way and it's hard to change one's habits. Our actions say, "I'm not willing to be patient; I'm not willing to develop our oneness." We feel that we have to compel the other person to do what we want. That hurts, so we criticize. And if our nagging and jabbing doesn't bring about a change, we feel that at least we've gotten our frustrations out and paid the other back a little bit for not pleasing us.

Possibly Vic, the husband just mentioned, explains his feelings about coming home and seeing utter chaos. For a while

Allison really tries to keep the house in order, but then it gets back to the same old mess. Vic feels that he tried the nice way but it didn't work. He decides to get tougher and let her know how sloppy she is, how hard he works, and that he has a right to expect a decent house to come home to, something to be proud of. He wants to make her feel guilty. She begins to dread his coming home at night.

At the root of the criticism is a conviction that each person has rights in marriage and that if those rights are not respected, then criticizing is not only a privilege but a responsibility. We're making marriage a "shaping up" process instead of a love affair. Marriage becomes a contract in which each party has to live up to certain terms. It ceases to be a relationship in which each is responsive to the other, trying to outdo him, not in demanding, but in *giving* as much of himself as possible.

A marriage based on criticism leads to minimalism. Each party gives only what he has to give, while trying to get all he can out of the other party.

There are other types of criticism. One includes blaming everything on a specific character defect. The opposite is the scatter type, in which each "mistake" is attributed to a different deficiency. Another is to base it on a person's sex— everything you do wrong is because you're a man—or a woman. There's no possible way that a person can arbitrarily change his sex. We can't deny what we are physically. But over the years of being criticized that way we become convinced something is basically wrong in being a man or a woman. We feel we have inherent characteristics that prevent us from being pleasing to our spouse.

Because we have set in our minds what men are like and what women are like, we ascribe those characteristics to our beloved even if there's little or no evidence of them. Allison may have erred in adding up the checkbook because the phone rang, or because she was rushing to pick Vic up at the station, or simply because she made a mistake. But Vic tells her she did it because women are no good with checkbooks. There's no way Allison can ever manage the checkbook to his satisfaction. Vic will always find something wrong because

I love you just exactly the way you are.

he's convinced that if a woman handles a checkbook, it can't ever come out right.

Allison may tell Vic that because he's a man he doesn't understand her. He throws up his hands in disgust—and despair —because no matter how much he reaches out to her, she's convinced that men just can't understand.

Do you use constructive criticism?   *Your answer:*

Constructive criticism is intended to be an honest concern for the good of another person. In marriage when we engage in constructive criticism, we suppose that we are aiming at helping our beloved live up to his potential, or we want him to be looked on favorably by other people.

Genuine constructive criticism involves gentleness and understanding. Bitterness and hostility have no part. We don't always accomplish with our criticism what we intend, because a lot of what we call constructive criticism is only a mask to allow us to get out our frustrations or put the other person down. This negative "constructive" criticism avoids some of the grosser deficiencies of destructive criticism, but it contains all the same elements of superiority, of passing judgments on another and of character assassination. For when we criticize "constructively," we often not only point out a mistake in word or action but we ascribe the mistake to a personality deficiency.

We say, "You know, dear, I'm saying this for your own good. You are awfully self-centered." Or—and we say these things with condescending smiles—"You're so good; in fact, you're just too good for this world." "You're so naive. People take advantage of you, so let me make the decisions." Or, "I know that you're very bright and have all sorts of talents, but you have so little taste in friends! Why don't you let me take care of our social life?" Or, "You're such a love, but you're a bull in a china shop and you always upset people when you talk. Why don't you—well—learn to be quiet?"

Such statements break down a person's morale. They have all the same deleterious effects on a person's self-confidence and self-image as blatant criticism. And it is sometimes more devastating when it's done nicely. When criticism is harsh, we have some protection in seeing that it's exaggerated or given because the other person has been hurt. When it's "constructive" we're sure to take it as a reality.

The worst thing about constructive criticism in a husband-and-wife relationship is that the criticizer puts himself outside the relationship. He stands apart, looking down at the other person, evaluating him, trying to teach him how to be a better person, how to improve as a spouse.

The result is that both discover areas where they consider themselves superior to the other. Each places himself in a teaching role. They look on this as part of their responsibility as husband or wife. It's a funny way to love each other, isn't it? It's not our responsibility as a married person to construct our spouse into anything! Our calling is to love the other person as he is.

What popular guise is there for criticism?

Your answer:

We all criticize, but none of us wants to be accused of doing it. So, to make sure we are not jumped on for being critical, we often clothe our barbs with teasing. We kid our husband or wife about something that he or she is doing and it's all very good-natured and ha-ha, but the point is relayed to the beloved that he has a defect. When he gets prickly about it, we say, "What's the matter? Can't you take a joke?" So we have it both ways. We get our point across and at the same time we make the other person feel guilty for acting disturbed. Actually we want our criticism to be taken seriously, but we offer it under the guise of humor.

This type of teasing criticism is really mean. It's tremendously frustrating, especially if we do it often. The other person never knows where he stands with us.

How much of your criticism is influenced by others?   *Your answer:*

It is likely that over the long run, people around us tend to increase our inclination to criticize our spouse. Our own families usually support us in our complaints. They encourage us to tell our spouse where we stand. And they don't want us to back down. Furthermore, other people tell us what they expect of a husband or a wife thereby giving us more things to criticize. They may say little things like, "Well, y'know I've been telling you all along that he isn't very reliable." Or, "I told you before you married her that she was all wrapped up in herself."

Our natural tendency to criticize is reinforced with the addition of each bit of new material. We watch carefully to see any evidence of certain traits cropping up in our partner.

Just as devastating are today's magazine articles and popular psychology books about marriage. The "rate-your-marriage" questionnaires make us feel insecure. They put into our heads all sorts of dissatisfactions that we never would have thought of. And the people we know who have the most to say about marriage are often the ones who are doing the least well in theirs. So the "experts" in any given neighborhood are the ones who are quite cynical.

Of course these people shouldn't receive all the blame. What do we communicate to them in the first place? A wife doesn't usually tell her neighbor, "My husband has a tremendous quality of listening. How can I get across to him how magnificent it is and how much I appreciate him?" No, but after one bad experience she's apt to go to the same neighbor and say, "My husband doesn't listen to me at all. How can I get him to listen?" A husband isn't inclined to talk much with his co-workers about how tender-hearted his wife is and how she lets him express himself, how concerned she is about his tensions, how she protects him from being overwhelmed by the difficulties of her day. He usually doesn't ask how he can demonstrate to her his awe for her goodness and love. No, but he will complain about the times she talks too much, adding that she certainly lacks understanding of a man's need for a little peace.

We do these things because we want the support of other people. We want them to agree with us, to back us up in criticizing our mate. We don't look for their support in helping us to recognize and appreciate the good qualities of our spouse, because we don't think we need any help in that area. Things are going fine. Fine for whom? Well, fine for us. But what about our beloved? Wouldn't some praise be appreciated? And worthwhile?

Considering our record of criticism and of praise, it would be important for us to go to others to learn how to give *praise*. We don't need any help in tearing down the other person. We're already very good at it. We need hints and insights to recognize how we can give meaningful credit to the one we love!

In what ways does your spouse know you better than anyone else?

Your answer:

68

Tonight we'll talk about how special we've been to each other this last year. Writing it down makes me realize how wonderful Russ is.

It's obvious that because we've been married 2 or 5 or 25 years, our husband or wife knows us better than anyone else.

We've done many things together, some of them secret, so no one else has experienced what we have. We also have an instinct for each other's likes and dislikes, recognizing reactions to different circumstances. We are able to read the telltale signs that each of us gives of being tired or angry or worried or bored, signs that anybody else would pass over.

We're also aware of each other's idiosyncrasies, weaknesses and failings. Over the years, we've become very conscious of the things that bother our spouse. Without a doubt, we would be able to name all the character and personality defects better than anyone else. We could give specific examples, including the ones we artfully hide from other people. This is to our shame. Isn't it a tragedy?

A husband looks at his bad qualities, expects his wife's displeasure and says, "See, she knows the worst about me and loves me anyway." A wife sees the worst in herself and says, "What a wonderful man he is; he accepts me with all my failings!" Wait a minute. Do we really want to be known for our shortcomings? Is that the "me" we were most conscious of the other's knowing when we first met, dated and were married? Did we really want to find someone who could discover the worst about us and want to marry us anyway? Did we try to find a person who would discover what was unattractive about us and still propose? No, what turned us on most to each other was how much we were appreciated and valued by the other person, how he saw—maybe better than we saw for ourselves—the goodness that was in us.

The goodness we had when we first met is still a part of us. In fact, now we have it in greater measure, because through our years together we have built up our habits of goodness and worth. In our early days together we would talk about how much each of us understood the other's ambitions and dreams, and how we recognized that we weren't as careless or as indifferent as we appeared to our family or others. We gave each other credit for being a wonderful person. Now, though, we feel that our spouse knows our bad qualities more than any others. Why?

The reason for this drastic change is criticism.

Sue and Carl, two dear friends of mine, considered themselves a very fortunate couple, able to say anything to each other. When Carl mentioned to Sue that she was spending too much time and attention on the children and ignoring him, things improved for quite awhile. If Sue told Carl that he was spending too much time watching television, TV got much less use for some time. No matter what it was, whether it was Carl having too much to drink at a party or Sue not treating his mother right, notice was taken of it and changes were made.

They had improved a great deal from their early days together. They had fewer fights and they were less intense, but something had gone out of their marriage. Finally they identified the problem. They were being very clear about what they didn't like about each other, but taking for granted what they liked. There wasn't as much tenderness as there had been and certainly not as much as they would like. The

I know how wonderful you are—how extra special!

71

only way that Carl knew when Sue was pleased with him was when she didn't have a gripe. Sue figured she must be all right in Carl's book as long as he didn't have a complaint.

They decided to start talking about the positive things, to praise each other for the good things. Sue discovered that Carl not only was a fair sort of fellow; he was positively good. Carl saw that Sue not only was willing to avoid doing anything to upset him, but was constantly doing things to please him. They recognized that when they first met they had instinctively seen the good qualities in each other and bypassed the bad qualities. Reversing that attitude had dampened their marriage. Getting into a positive attitude again put the old sparkle—and a new one—into being married.

Isn't it true that during your dating and engagement days you rarely criticized each other? Instead you praised each other. You brought out the affection that was in your hearts. You didn't talk much about where you were wrong. You talked about where you were right, where you respected and admired each other.

The point is not whether we analyzed each other's character accurately or not. The point is how we saw each other. I saw the best in you. You saw the best in me. And we were rich because of it. Unfortunately, now we are convinced that the other person is more alert to our defects. Neither one of us thinks much about good points. They are taken for granted. Somehow we tend to believe that anyone can know our good points, but only a husband or wife can know our bad points.

Actually, only our beloved has experienced our good points to the degree and depth of which we are capable. It is our beloved who has experienced our goodness more frequently and more meaningfully than anyone else.

What is the best thing to do about criticism?   *Your answer:*

The best thing we can do about criticism is to totally remove it from our lifestyle. Criticism adds absolutely nothing to our self-appreciation, our appreciation of our spouse, or the beauty of our relationship. Being critical makes us judgmental and gives us an attitude of superiority. It makes us set up our relationship in terms of how well each one is living up to the expectations of the other.

The worst effect of criticism is that it makes my beloved less clear about his own goodness and worth. It tears down his self-esteem, leading him to hold back because he doesn't want to be open for further criticism. Even if criticism leads to some kind of improvement in what is being done, it doesn't lead to an improvement of the person's responsiveness. It leads to withdrawal rather than increased closeness. Response is forced and grudging rather than free and eager.

Criticism leads to a relationship in which one person is working—continually working—to build the other into his own image and likeness, rather than accepting the other as he is and rejoicing in the uniqueness of his personhood.

Criticism is "I-centered." I'm looking for my own satisfaction. I'm wanting you to change in order to please me. I want you to fit into *my* plans for our marriage.

For some strange reason we believe that criticism is the only way we can accomplish a change in our mate. Even though criticism doesn't accomplish anything but hurt and coolness in our own lives, we feel that it will motivate the other person to change! But the highest motivation for him to change is an awareness of his love for us.

Realizing that should make us reluctant to criticize, but it doesn't. Deep down our conviction is that if we don't criticize, we'll have to give up any hope for improvement in our relationship. We're actually thinking that our being displeased creates a stronger motivation than our being pleased; that our beloved will react better to our being unhappy with him than to our being happy. Our criticizing shows how insecure we are. We must feel unloved—or unlovely, so we use the whip of criticism in order to get things our way.

Most of us have no conception of how large a part criticism plays in our lives. Criticism is so natural that we do it

73

Hey, thanks for being you. I'm sure glad we're "us."

without thinking. If our spouse says to us, "You're criticizing me," we're liable to say, "No, I was just making a comment." We don't label our criticism as criticism! It would be a good idea for all of us to take a piece of paper and pencil, look over the past week and write down the criticisms we have made of our beloved. Don't rationalize, give excuses or explanations. Don't eliminate any comments on the basis that they were taken in good humor or seemed to be appreciated!

Total up the criticisms expressed, including the subtle and implied—even the unspoken—as well as the obvious and harsh. Include a raised eyebrow or a tone of voice, and the criticisms we consider to be justified as well as those in which we went too far. The point is not whether we had reason to be critical, it's whether we criticized. If we list only a few criticisms for a whole week, then we'd better look within ourselves, because more than likely we're not aware of what our words have been. Maybe we'd better ask our spouse to write a list for us so that we know what's happening. If we don't

74

recognize when and how frequently we're criticizing, we're never going to change.

The next step is to declare a moratorium on criticism. We should decide that for 30, 60 or 90 days there will be *no criticism*. This is not something we ease into. It's like giving up cigarettes. It has to be cold turkey.

We know that at times we'll fail, and we are not to hold that against each other. But we'll honestly and sincerely put all our efforts into avoiding criticism of each other for a specific length of time. We must agree to help each other. We may set up a little signal, such as a thumb held up, or a special code word to let the other person know he's criticizing.

Committing ourselves to a period of *no criticism* means more than holding back critical words or actions. For if we just hold in our criticisms for an extended period of time, it can lead to a major blowup. Rather, we are to kill our critical spirit by concentrating on the good qualities of our beloved. We have to force ourselves to be prepared against the poison which festers within us by consciously seeing the worthy qualities of our beloved.

Let us commit ourselves to a certain number of days of no criticism no matter how long it takes us to reach that number. Only the days without criticism count. If we fail on a given day by inferring that our spouse is not very considerate or whatever—that day doesn't count. So I may get through the first day without criticizing, but then the second day I sure let her know she forgot to buy light bulbs. That day doesn't count. So, if I make it through the next day, keeping in mind how much she's done for me, it becomes day number two. It may take me 180 days to get my 30, 60 or 90 in, but every one of those days is for the bettering of our relationship.

Meg, a youthful wife in a midwestern parish, was determined to cut out criticizing her husband, Paul. She didn't notice much of a change in their relationship at the beginning, so it was difficult not be begin criticizing again. But about halfway through Paul said to her, "Hey, honey, you're so different. What's happening?" When she told him he started to try, too. It was just wonderful. It was like getting a completely fresh start on their marriage. In the 90 days, all kinds of things happened! Paul smiled more and more. He came home earlier—at 5:30 every night, where for a number of years it had been 6:30 or 7:00. But the biggest change had happened in Meg. She didn't feel angry and put upon anymore. She loved being married to Paul!

Without a doubt, we should eliminate criticism. We shouldn't just be nicer, more gentle, or take into consideration the other person's feelings and criticize less. We should unequivocally *stop criticizing!*

What would happen if you didn't criticize your loved one?

Your answer:

Do we think that if we don't criticize our spouse, she will get away with too much, that he'll get worse than he is already? Are we afraid we'll look like a patsy?

We ought to feel encouraged to try something different when we consider our lack of success in criticizing. After all, we've been doing it for a long time. Can we say that it's worked out all that well? Have we really gained what we've wanted? Have we accomplished anything? Is he more thoughtful? Has she become more punctual? The only thing we've gained by all the criticism we've poured out is some vented frustrations and maybe a decision or two. By stopping that hurtful negativism and giving up our right to criticize for a while, we'll gain much more!

Of course if we don't like the results of the lack of criticism, we can always go back to criticizing. If we consider "life without criticism" to be valueless, if we're not getting enough out of being approving, then we won't have lost all that much practice in being critical. We can get our critical spirit back very quickly. We've been working hard at it for 5, 10 or 30 years, so to give it up for 30 to 90 days isn't going to interfere much with our skill in the matter!

What we can hope to gain is a sparkle instead of a hurt in our spouse's eyes, a smile on his lips instead of grim lines around his mouth, a surprised "Do you mean it?" instead of a heavy "I'm sorry."

Freedom from criticism brings a lightness into the atmosphere, a greater openness and responsiveness and an opportunity to really enjoy each other's company more than ever before. The *no criticism* pledge brings the security of knowing that we're not going to be put on the spot.

Being allowed to be ourselves and responding to each other because we want to and not because we have to is a wonderful and marvelous experience.

I often visit Fran and Paul. They have a good marriage, and they are determined to keep it that way. They have worked hard on it over their 12 years together. They have always prided themselves on being very open with each other. If either one had a gripe he came out with it.

A while back I wondered out loud to them if maybe they were doing all the right things but missing what each other was really about. I knew it was important to correct defects and to continually do better by each other, but it seemed to me that it was even more important to appreciate each other.

Paul told me later that they'd agreed with me. They had worked so hard at improving each other they hadn't really enjoyed each other spontaneously—with excitement.

Then, for one solid month they had just talked about what they noticed in each other that pleased them. They had begun to tell each other how much they appreciated each other's goodness. It was really great, and one night they'd heard the clincher. Terry, their oldest daughter, had said, "Wow, this is a different house. You two aren't so serious anymore. It's fun to be part of this family!"

Reversing our thinking, we will be amazed at how much more positively we look at each other, how much more we find goodness and richness spotlighted. When we are approved of, we are lighthearted and joyous. When we receive disapproval we become heavy and plodding. When criticism is absent, romance has a chance to enter our lives. We have an opportunity to develop our good points, to rejoice in potentials we only dimly realized we had. We can be relaxed and at ease! Loving, we can enjoy living!

I love being married to you, Honey!

79

We're the happiest people in the whole world.

TOUCHING YOU MAKES YOUR CENTRAL BEING MORE PRESENT TO ME THAN WHAT WE ARE TALKING ABOUT.

BODY LANGUAGE

How much do you touch each other now?   *Your answer:*

When a young couple dates they talk and talk about what their married life is going to be like. They talk about where they're going to live, how many children they're going to have, what kind of family they're going to have, some of their fears, places they're going to visit. It seems they talk about everything, and most of it is based on assumptions. They assume that their relationship and their communication is going to remain the same or get better when they're married. Because they want to spend all their time together, they feel they will always listen to each other with the same eagerness and enthusiasm.

When a couple is dating or first married, they're always touching. It is such a thrill to hold hands that it doesn't enter either one's mind that they might not be touching with the same frequency and sensitivity in later years. He loves to hold her face in his hands; she loves to run her fingers through his hair. It means so much!

But a few years of being married brings about a change.

Whether it's walking along the street, being at a party or just sitting in the living room, it's not in a couple's minds to make a point of touching. Aren't their hands always occupied with a newspaper, a cigarette, a book or something? Or aren't they often sitting out of touching range—and not doing anything about it? Walking along on the street, they are more comfortable keeping their hands in their pockets or letting them swing freely. When a husband comes home from work, he might give his wife a quick hug and a peck and then busy his hands with opening mail. She's much too concerned with the dinner to want to be distracted by being touched. Even if one is affectionate and gives the other a hug, it may be shrugged off or dismissed by a stiffening of the back muscles or a patient waiting out of the squeeze, communicating that touching is not particularly appreciated.

What's happened? When you were dating you were always close beside each other whether you were in the car or on the couch or in the kitchen or wherever. Maybe you want to go back to that kind of relationship—it was so beautiful—but you don't bring it up because you think the other person is content with the way things are. Or maybe you've talked about it and it's a sore spot, so you've let it drop. Or is it that both of you are satisfied to have touching out of your lives? Another possibility is that neither of you has given it much thought. If so, it is important to take notice of what has happened, to recognize the difference in your nonverbal communication from the first years of your love and now. You may want your lifestyle to change!

What effect does less touching have on your communication?

Your answer:

84

You're coming through to me loud and clear.

When a couple is close together touching, they sense each other. It's very different than just talking. A space between two people adds a certain amount of objectivity. We recognize that when we're dealing with people at work or elsewhere. Touching is too intimate. We might shake hands or give someone a quick hug and a kiss and then we stay apart to talk.

There's a definite involvement when we're touching or being touched, so when we're not touching the other person, there is an apartness. The space brings about an impersonal relationship. No matter how tender and understanding we were in the past, when we're not touching, a special element of oneness is absent. A couple doesn't have to be touching each other every single moment they are together, but when touching is less frequent, a certain gentleness and tenderness goes out of their relationship.

It's hard not to listen to somebody when you're touching. It's difficult to become absorbed in someone with only your eyes and ears. You need your hands. All of us have experienced moments when we knew that the other person wasn't there. He could answer us correctly and repeat everything we said and yet wasn't with us. Being in tune can take place if we're not holding hands or our arms aren't around each other, but it's less likely. Touching gives us a real feeling for each other.

Most of all, touching takes us beyond ourselves to the other person. When I'm touching you, my mind is going to you. It's harder for me to concentrate on just myself—on what I am saying or what's going on within me. This is true, isn't it? When we want to look inside ourselves, when we want to find out what we are thinking or want to soak in an experience that's going on within ourselves, we pull apart from people. So the decrease in touching indicates a cooling off of a relationship, a person's greater involvement with his own interests.

Another effect of less frequent touching is increased sensitivity to being hurt. We feel isolated, not understood, taken for granted—and sometimes used. Marriage can become a chore. We perform our role, not out of pleasure, but because we have to. Our sense of personal relationship suffers.

We feel that our time of romance is gone, that it used to be in our lives, but now it's for younger people. It isn't necessarily that we're dissatisfied or upset or angry with each other or that we're not willing to live up to the responsibilities we assumed in marriage, but the sparkle has gone out of it. It's flat. We have our focus on other things rather than on each other. We "lose touch" by our lack of touch.

Why do you touch less?   *Your answer:*

Why does a wife sit on the far side of the car seat? She doesn't say, "I don't want you to touch me any more," but she's more comfortable if she puts her elbow on the arm rest. Why does a husband come home at night, hug and kiss his wife and turn away from her? He wants to read the paper or listen to the news before supper. We're always available to each other, so in a way we're seldom really available. We touch less because we've grown used to each other. There isn't the newness we had before marriage. The wonder of being understood and being responded to has disappeared.

Actually we've been trained to feel that holding hands is just for young lovers, that after the honeymoon, romance ends, at least in public. Why then do we also stop holding hands in the privacy of our own homes? Why can a person go into a restaurant and almost always tell who's married and who's not? Those who are holding hands and looking at each other are not married!

It isn't that somebody holds a gun on us and forbids us to hold hands any more, but maybe somebody at a party saw us holding hands and said sardonically, "Aren't they sweet?" So, gradually we stopped holding hands because we didn't want to be "sweet."

However, we may be among those married couples who still hold hands, but the meaning is gone. It's something we do like putting on our gloves or overshoes. It's comfortable. Yes, we're holding hands, but we're scarcely touching. There's no dynamic, no attention being given to it. There's nothing "coming through" between us.

It may be that we don't touch each other any more because we're not so absorbed in each other as at first and we're busy with other things. Our whole life doesn't center around "us" —the way it did when we were dating. We have a time and a place for everything. Now there are all sorts of things we have to fit into our day. We fit us and our relationship into the leftover time.

Another reason why we don't touch each other much is that it just doesn't seem to be convenient. When we were dating, we'd hold hands even if our hands froze. We'd keep our

Nobody's looking our way—here's a special kiss. X

arms around each other even if we'd get an ache in our neck. Now it's more important to be comfortable. Furthermore, we don't think we have time. It was one thing when we were dating; we had all the time in the world. It's another thing now. We have allowed distractions to creep in. While we excuse ourselves on the basis that there's not much we can do about it, there's actually a lot we can do about it. If we don't, it's because we choose to let other things be more important. We have each other, we think. Isn't that enough?

There are many jokes about how men and women let themselves go after marriage. People figure they've found their mates and don't have to do anything to keep them, that the other person is stuck. We see cartoons of the woman who was light and lively and lithesome in her 20's and is now fat and 40. There is the guy who was always well-dressed and took good care of his hair and is now sitting around in a sweaty undershirt, with rumpled hair. It's probably safe to say that neither cares any longer what the other person thinks.

It's the same as far as touching is concerned. We don't care what the other person thinks or feels.

In the first case, we've let ourselves go. In the second case, we've let the other person go! We're not holding on. We figure that they'll always be beside us no matter what we do.

When touching is part of the tone of our lives we're saying that we're involved, we're giving ourselves to each other. When we keep our hands off each other, we're saying that we're keeping ourselves to ourselves—we'd rather be about our own business.

Do you consider touching a form of communication?

Your answer:

Touching is more than an incidental action that makes us feel better. There is a certain amount of comfort and security involved in it—and some affection being expressed—but more than that, it's necessary for communication.

Communication isn't only speaking and listening. For when thoughts are audible and clearly stated; even when they are heard, comprehended and responded to, another dimension increases their effectiveness. That added factor is touching.

Touching is an important aspect of any communication, but especially between a husband and wife. There are many things that can be understood only when they are touching.

I may visit a couple who are going through a difficult experience with their children. I can say all the beautiful things and pour my heart out to show how much I care, how much I'm suffering with them. And it may not reach them. But if I put my arms around them, they sense the compassion and gentleness and understanding in what I'm trying to say.

It isn't only in extreme circumstances but in normal, everyday circumstances that touching is meaningful. Preparing meal after meal, washing dishes and wiping up tables after kids' meals can be a dreary existence. A husband's squeeze can say more to a wife than any words possibly can. Going to work day after day and getting chopped up in the rat race, living through the strain of holding a job, trying to get ahead and worrying about the family can be a terrible drain on a husband. A wife can say she knows what he is going through, but it can come across as only an intellectual understanding with no personal involvement. It is when she holds him that he can experience her awareness and appreciation of him.

In this respect Gil wanted me to share his experience. A particular suppertime made him aware of his wife's touch. He'd had a hard day at work and the evening traffic was bad on the freeway. Things had been no better when he approached his own driveway and saw Billy's bike. It was always something. He pretty much grumped his way through supper. He knew he wasn't being fair to Cathy and the kids, but he just couldn't seem to help himself. Slowly he became aware that Cathy was going out of her way to touch him.

Waiting, watching for the children, your back feels so good.

She'd pat him on the arm or put her hand against his cheek or give him a quick hug when she got up to get something for the table. At first, he didn't want to even notice it, but then he realized that he liked it. He even hoped that she'd have to get something more from the kitchen. Gradually, he felt the poison of the day oozing out of him. His muscles relaxed and he started to become more himself. He pulled her to him, "Cathy, I love you. Stay close. Your touch works wonders in me."

A simple brushing against your beloved, a quick touch, a gentle pat, can warm him more than all the words in the world. He feels he's been noticed, thought and cared about, assured that he matters. A storm may be stirring inside him or a bitterness eating at him which can be better touched away than talked away.

And joy and exultation are not emotions we enjoy only alone. We want to share them. A football team in its exuberance of winning slaps each other on the back and lifts the captain into the air. How about a girl who announces her engagement? The other girls have to hug her and see the ring. They don't just look at the ring, they hold her hand to share her happiness. It is the same thing when a special joy comes into the life of a husband and wife. They can't get the fullness of it without touching each other. The experience that's vibrant inside them has to pour out through their bodies as well as their mouths.

Is one of you the toucher?

Your answer:

In a husband-and-wife relationship one person is likely to be more of the touching type than the other. The one may have grown up in a family where they showed their affection to one another openly, so it is easy and natural for him to touch and be touched. The other may have grown up in a family where they didn't, so it's very difficult for him to touch or accept touches. To that person, touching is considered too demonstrative.

Part of the problem is in the very words we use to describe this. We say that the one who touches is more affectionate than the other. We confine touching to affection. There's no question that touching expresses affection—tenderness, gentleness, warmth—and that's all fine and good, but actually it goes far beyond that. Our hands have a much broader vocabulary. The person who is eager to touch is one who is putting his attention on the other person and wants the other person to be attentive in return. We just don't touch anybody! Therefore, we're assuming a certain amount of intimacy, a certain amount of participation in the life of the other by touching.

There's also a security brought about by our touching. We trust each other. I'm encouraged, freed to tell you what is going on inside me. So while affection may be present in our touching, my fingers may be signaling my need of your help to get out what I have to say. Or I may have noticed that you are under duress and I want to calm you.

Have you ever wondered why people like to have pets and plants? It is probably because we can touch them. Instinctively, we want to touch something, and the beautiful thing about pets and plants is that they are available. They are there and we can touch them without getting involved. We wouldn't conceive of having a cat or a dog without touching it, because that's the major way of people-animal communication. Touching is also important for person-to-person communications. Just because people can talk to one another doesn't mean that touching and other forms of communication are unneeded.

We often look on the "touchers" as being a bit weak, not having the strength to keep their emotions to themselves. But the opposite is the case. They have courage. The ones who keep everything inside, who don't reach out and touch, are the ones who are weak. They don't want to be exposed. They don't want others to know them, so they put on a front of being impervious to difficulties or dangers.

One of the beautiful things about a couple relationship is that each has special strengths and gifts that the other person gradually takes on. A wife senses her husband's gentleness and gradually becomes more gentle herself. A husband senses his wife's understanding and becomes more understanding himself. The person who doesn't have the gift of touching

Your touch electrifies me, calms me, assures me of your love.

can learn to appreciate it in the beloved and gradually acquire it. Too, the person who has the gift of touching can tenderly pull the partner out of being uptight, closed or unwilling to be demonstrative.

Or maybe a father is a big help. One night after Karen's folks had been over for dinner and she and Dave were finishing up in the kitchen, it hit him why he enjoyed them. "Karen, your mom and dad are like newlyweds. He's always holding her hand or has his arm around her. She leans her head against his shoulder."

"They've been that way ever since I was a little girl," replied Karen.

"I guess I'm jealous of your dad," confessed Dave. "I love you and I want to be a good husband, but I don't think I'm anywhere near as gentle and loving with you as your dad is with your mom. Your dad gave me some advice tonight. He told me that if my hands were ever cut off, you'd never miss them. He said I'd have to tell you they were gone. He said he wanted me to know that love has to be hand-delivered.

"He has something there, but I feel like a school boy. This is ridiculous. We've been married 15 years and I feel awkward holding your hand or putting my arm around you. Here, how's this for a start?" Dave gave her a squeeze.

A couple months later when Karen's folks were over again, Karen said to her dad, "Your advice to Dave was great. Thanks, Dad. I thought we were beyond what we called the soupy stage. I'm so glad we're not. It's a whole new life!"

When you hold hands, what are you saying?   *Your answer:*

We have the idea that holding hands is just "holding hands," that a hug is just a "hug." But neither is a simple thing, it is complex. We send all sorts of messages to each other through our hands and arms.

Patty, a young wife in a couple's group, mentioned a little incident that had meant a great deal to her. She and her husband, Danny, had come out from a movie the Saturday night before and were walking along the street towards home when she hesitantly put her hand in his pocket to hold his hand. Other times Danny had pulled out a handkerchief to blow his nose and then didn't put his hand back in his pocket or he lit a cigarette or he just took his hand out and gestured as he talked.

This time he left his hand in his pocket. She felt the size of Danny's hand and the strength of his fingers. It made her feel safe, protected. This was the best part of the evening. There was magic in the moment as his hand relaxed in hers. She didn't say very much. She just wanted to enjoy the feeling of his hand. It was so, so nice. Patty hoped it would happen often.

We also communicate the intensity of our feelings or the depth of our conviction by how firmly we hold the other person. We show the extent of our consciousness of the other person by the particular quality of our touch. Through the way we hold hands we can plead for understanding. We can touch the other person back to life after a particular hurt, or seek forgiveness.

The trembling of the fingertips, the coldness of a hand, the sweatiness of a palm, the goosebumps on the arm, the tension of our body muscles, express deep inner feelings.

We may communicate to our spouse much of which we are not aware. Our words, for example, might express anger and hostility, and demand that the other person recognize that he's been treating us wrongly. Yet our hands might be pleading for understanding and forgiveness, closeness and warmth. We might be driving our beloved away with our speech and at the same time trying to draw him close with our touch. Or we may say everything is all right between us, but a stiffened back indicates it's not. We're sending out contradictory signals. Actually our beloved is clued in on where we are. Although we may be saying one thing with our mouths and another thing with our hands, it's usually our hands that are the most accurate.

There are times we don't intend to be delivering a message at all. We happen to feel close, so we hold our beloved's hand or give him a particularly warm hug or a tender caress, and that's as far as it goes. But that's underestimating our capacity. We're not taking advantage of a wonderful opportunity to communicate. We can make those moments mean something. They can be beautiful, enhancing our relationship. They are "we" moments.

A traditional cartoon about marriage shows the husband at the breakfast table drinking his coffee and reading the newspaper while his wife is standing there in robe and slippers, her hair in curlers. She's chattering away and saying to him, "But you're not listening to me," and he says, "But you're not saying anything." They're both right!

I need you all the time. Thanks for caring.

What are we saying with our good morning or have-a-good-day kiss, or our welcome home hug and good-night squeeze? If we go through the ritual because we think that's what's expected of a husband and wife and then pour out what happened during the day, we haven't intended to say anything. However, we're communicating a great deal. We're telling our spouse that our greetings don't mean much. We're repeating the habit because the other person expects it of us or because it's the proper thing to do. I'm saying, "Now that it's over with, we'll get down to the real communication. I want to tell you what went on today." Wait a minute! It's more important to take care of the relationship, making it dominant, than it is to have a rundown of the day's events. You and I—we—are more important than anything else. And our hands can help us say that. Let us touch each other with the full awareness of our relationship.

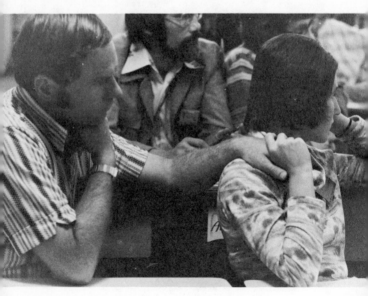

Your hand feels so strong. You're terribly important to me.

If a husband is feeling warm and tender toward his wife, then he wants her to hold his hand or put her arms around him. He's saying, "This is the way I'm feeling, so I want you to feel the same way. Express it to me outwardly by your touch or kiss or hug." Therefore the only message she can deliver to him—if she touches him under those circumstances—is the one he's already set up to hear. If she doesn't, she's not listening to him at all. We can only change the mood that our spouse is wanting to create by avoiding any touching or by holding hands without any meaning.

Sometimes I don't allow you to touch me because I'm not in the mood for it. The fact that you want to communicate to me through your hands is irrelevant. I'm not up to it. I'm not interested—and you are not to expect me to be interested. We don't accept that attitude as far as verbal communication is concerned. If our beloved wants to speak, we are supposed to listen. We may not always do it, but we know we should. Nonverbal communication is every bit as important or more so.

Touching is normal and natural between a husband and wife, especially when they're feeling good about each other, and it goes beyond that. So we can try to keep our fingers tuned in, in the same way we try to keep our ears tuned in to each other. We can try to pick out what the other person means by what he's saying with his hands. We can decipher what our beloved is saying by his rubbing his thumb on the back of our hand. What is the looseness of the grip saying? What question is the hug asking? What meaning is the pressure of the lips expressing?

As we tune ourselves in to nonverbal communication, we can experience our spouse in stereo.

Does the other person know what you are saying?

In the same way that we care about our verbal communication getting across, we should care about our nonverbal communication.

I can be very clear in my own mind what I'm communicating with my hands, but I can't expect someone else to automatically understand. If my beloved doesn't get my message I can't say, "Well, if you don't know, then you don't care." That simply is not true. Even if it were true, it's no excuse for me to give up.

I have to ask myself how I can best transmit my feelings through my hands, my body, to my spouse. So I have to be looking for clues, verbal and nonverbal, from him to discover if what I'm expressing is getting across or not. Maybe I have to change my nonverbal communication a little—or a lot—to be understood. Maybe my body language is being misunderstood or it isn't adequate in itself, so I should add some verbal communication.

When Dotty was going to give a talk to a large group, she'd be tense, her hands would be ice cold and she wanted to be held close for a bit. She enjoyed speaking but was fearful beforehand. Joe commented that the nights she went out suppertime was awkward and he felt ornery. One night as Dotty was getting ready she talked about it to Joe. "Honey, I need your arms around me. Do you feel how knotted up I am in my back? That's exactly the way my stomach is and it's the way my heart is too. My hands are cold and I'm edgy. I'll be okay as soon as I get going. But right now—for a moment—hold me tight." From then on Joe had a part in her speaking engagements, and they both felt better.

Perhaps our nonverbal communication is so "I" centered

that the message is confused. We may need to help our spouse to be predisposed to our feelings in the way Dotty helped Joe.

It is difficult, too, for the other person to know what we mean if we seldom accept his touch. If I keep to myself for long stretches of time, I can't expect the other person to be cued in to me. If touching is strictly only when I feel like it, it's not real communication. That's using my spouse. That's putting him at my disposal, making communication not an interchange, but a request for services.

As we make sure that our touching conveys what we intend it to, we will have our own private language that will grow and develop to be continually more exciting and more satisfying.

What effect does touching have on your verbal communication?

Your answer:

A contour map tells more than a flat map. A stereoscope gives depth to two-dimension pictures. Similarly, touching adds to a couple's experience. It intensifies one's attentiveness to what is being said and brings the other person alive. It adds nuances to what is being said and encourages the other person as he talks. It's a sign that we care, that we're interested in giving or receiving the fullness of what is being said.

Touching says to our beloved that he is not just anybody, but someone in whom we have a stake; he belongs to us. We have a very special relationship. An intimacy is brought about that is not present in verbal communication alone. Touching reassures our beloved, telling him he can be his full self with us.

When a couple is holding each other, they're able to say difficult things without hurting each other. Their touching shows caring. Even though they may be saying things that could be abrasive, the healing is simultaneous.

There is another very personal aspect to touching. Even the most mundane topic becomes something out of the ordinary, because it's for just the two of them.

What effect does nonverbal communication have on your sexual communication?

Your answer:

Difficulties are caused when couples make the mistake of assuming that because they're having sex they don't need to be touching each other as they did before they got married. They think that going to bed has replaced the need for nonverbal communication.

However, to be honest about it, people have engaged in sex before marriage and that didn't interfere with their holding hands or putting their arms around each other at other times. It was only after marriage that they suddenly decided that sex had replaced touching.

Part of the reason is a self-fulfilling prophecy. Many people think that touching is only a prelude to sexual involvement. When they don't want sex, they feel it's not a time for nonverbal communication. So, in touching, the implicit communication says: "We're going to go all the way." This leads to a wife feeling about her husband that all he wants is one thing, and saying to him, "You only touch me when you want sex." (We often put the blame on the other person when actually we're involved in creating the situation. We, ourselves, limit our touching. A wife may complain to the husband that it used to be so nice when they went any place because they always sat so close in the car and now they don't. He can simply ask her, "Who moved?"

One problem in connecting touching only with sex is that sex becomes a less important part of our lives. It becomes an activity rather than an opportunity to communicate our love.

Sex is strong medicine. We need to prepare for it. If we haven't touched each other all day, it's overwhelming to suddenly dive into sex at night. We tend to consider it an act to be performed rather than another way to relate to each other.

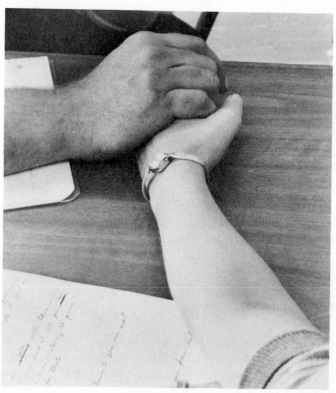

Your touch is what makes my day.

103

Touching can be integrated into the whole day and not kept as only a preliminary to sexual activity. When a couple is accustomed to experiencing each other verbally and physically, then sex fits into the total picture. Sex becomes a part of their expression of themselves to each other, rather than just something to do together with mutual approval and pleasure.

One of the difficulties in life is that people segregate the many aspects of their lives. They have their everyday routine, their spiritual life, their sexual life, their life as parents, their social life, the life with the relatives, the life with the commu-

You're tense, Darling.

Lean against me. My love is here for you.

nity. It would be better to look at the many aspects of life as parts of a whole. We have *one* life with various opportunities to express our relationship to each other and our mutual relationship to others. When I partition off these aspects, I focus in on what I'm doing rather than on you. I concentrate on the fact that I'm going to visit your mother, that I'm dealing with our children, that I have responsibilities to our neighbor, that I'm going to engage in sex, or I have civic responsibilities. I act as a separate individual who happens to be accompanying you during these activities. Even in a man and woman's sexual relationship, they are doing something together that's pleasurable rather than sharing their personhood.

Nonverbal communication is very important in sex. If we can be fully present to each other through touching we can expect sex to become a means of listening to each other, the greatest way of all to be open with each other.

Each day is made up of a lot of little things to share with each other. They add up to the whole picture of our relationship. If we only share big things, soon only those big things are meaningful to us. Everything else, in our eyes, is colorless. Actually we are depriving our life of much depth and texture. Furthermore, without sharing the little things during the day, there are many opportunities to misunderstand each other in the evening. We need to be communicating verbally and nonverbally often during the day.

Most of us are good, solid, everyday persons and the things that are meaningful to us would not make headlines, but as we talk them over and deal with them they have significance for us. Life with all of its ups and downs has zest because we are in tune with each other. Sex is not routine when we are in harmony, when we're prepared for each other by our nonverbal as well as our verbal communication. When we are not in physical contact, sex can become too important because it has to carry the burden for all our physical communication with each other. Or it may become less important than it should be because it's too big to cope with without on-going nonverbal communication. So we make it just routine—something we can take as an everyday type of thing.

Do you listen to your spouse's body language?

The more alert a husband and wife are to each other, the more they can tell what's going on. They can be aware of the meaning of the heavy footstep on the stairs, the sudden way he removes his tie, the careless way she takes off her coat. Sometimes a telltale vein on a hand or on a forehead lets them know there's something wrong inside their beloved. A lack of makeup or a desire to go to sleep right after dinner, mussed hair or drumming fingers, can clue in the listening mate.

Sometimes we're so busy about our own things that we don't notice the bits of evidence. We may only reflect afterwards and say, "Yes, I should have known that she was worried." "I should have realized that he had a hard day."

Any time we're bound up in ourselves, we don't want to listen. It's only when we've had a pretty good day, that we can notice the other person. If we've had a bad day, we want to be noticed. When we do notice, there often are barriers to our responding. We're rushing to go someplace, or we want to get dinner on the table, or we want to read the newspaper or watch the news. We hope that in a little while the other person will have snapped out of it or taken care of it for himself. Or maybe we're in a bad mood and remember that the last time we were miserable, he didn't notice.

On the whole, though, we know when our beloved is upset, and we want to make some kind of effort to help him. We may do it indirectly, by shooing the kids away or by trying to be particularly light and lively. That may help some, but the best thing is to sit down and talk it out. It may be harder. It means we have to get involved. But if we do it, we won't be bypassing a magnificent opportunity to get closer to each other.

Sometimes when a person is down he engages in the kind of body language that we don't particularly approve of, so we tend to avoid talking out the problem. He may become very short-tempered, pick at the children, brood by himself or go off to sleep. Because we're uneasy, instead of listening to his body language we react negatively, in terms of how it's affecting us. We pay attention to what his activity is doing to us. If we can forget ourselves and focus in on the person who matters more to us than any one else in the world, we'll catch his message.

Are you aware of your own body language?   *Your answer:*

Our emotions are complicated and a couple relationship is complex, so we may be expressing something through our body language that we don't know we're saying. Or, we're saying one thing with our words and another thing with our body. The surprising thing is that we're usually not even aware of a contradiction! At other times we intend to send out a strong message through our body posture and movements, contradicting it with our words—or lack of words— because we want our spouse to guess what's going on inside of us. Then when he doesn't know exactly why we're acting the way we are, we get upset.

Being aware of our own body language can help us see ourselves. It would be good if we could be conscious of just where we are at any given time and what we're saying to our spouse. Let's try. Let's not only hear what our spouse is saying to us, but understand what we're saying—verbally and nonverbally!

107

Do you look at your spouse when listening?

It hurts our relationship when we listen to our husband or wife with only half an ear. It's even worse when we don't give them any eye at all! Of course we're occupied. Our concern is with the normal household chores of picking up things, washing dishes, fixing up something about the house. Our eyes are busy everywhere. But maybe we just look down at our shoes or over the other person's shoulder or out the window.

Why? We can't be fully present to the other person unless we have our eyes on him and allow him to look into us. That's just it! Looking at the other person is difficult because we see into him and we find it too intimate to have him see into us! The eyes are the window of the soul, so we generally keep them shaded.

But in our couple relationship we need to see into each other. We can pick up much by eye contact that we cannot pick up through our ears or hands. We're more personal, more conscious of the other person, more aware of "us."

Have you ever had the experience of talking casually with someone as you're doing something about the house and suddenly it registers with you that the person is very upset? It's then that you see something going on inside him, so you stop cold, make eye contact and get absorbed in him. Beforehand you were hearing the words, but now you're looking at the person and responding to him in depth. It makes a big difference.

Examine your normal conversation with each other. Do you look at each other frequently? Just as we've discovered that our hands are generally occupied with something other than our beloved, we may find that our eyes are too. We may not have made a conscious effort to avoid looking at the

The curve of your cheek makes me alive to you.
Tracing your face thrills me.

other person, except when we're upset and don't want him to see into us, but we just don't let our eyes meet his.

Because of our busy way of living, we need to make a deliberate, conscious effort to stand still and look at the other person. When we're engaged in everyday communication, we're busy—often with our backs to each other.

It isn't essential to always be close, hold hands and look at each other to talk. Routine conversation allows for a casual approach, but there's a great need in a husband-and-wife relationship for deeper communication. We need to decide to build this type of communication and start doing it on a daily basis.

We mustn't leave it until something big is going on between us. Then our relationship is determined by outside circumstances or events. We need to start now, for the most important thing we can do is to concentrate on developing our awareness of each other. And giving *us* priority means taking some time on a daily basis to be in communion with each other, aware of body language, touching and looking into each other's soul.

Are your topics of conversation different when you are touching?

Your answer:

I wish for us—never to forget our first anniversary.

The more aware we are of each other, the more personalized the topic of conversation tends to be. Even an event or a principle can become personal—a platform on which to stand and look into each other.

When we are fully engaged with each other, hands, eyes, mouth, ears, we are sensitive to each other. We are less objective, more subjective. We are more caring, more responsive. There is less emphasis on getting our point across, more willingness to listen.

When we're not touching or looking at each other we tend to keep ourselves apart. We stay absorbed in our own point of view. When we are touching and looking at each other, the overriding topic of conversation is *us*. We put *us* in the spotlight. We're conscious of how important we are to each other.

When was the last time you traced each other's face with your fingertips?

Your answer:

Sometimes the simplest things are the most significant. Outlining each other's face is deeply meaningful for lovers. It has a profound effect on the toucher and the touched. We blot out everything else and concentrate on us.

We may not consider ourselves very talented lovers for we think we need the imagination of a genius or the talent of a poet to express love in glowing terms. But very little imagination or genius is really needed to love. It's our hands that can mean much.

Just take a few minutes, get comfortable together and trace each other's face. You'll go apart with the memory of each other embedded in your hearts. You have placed your identity on your spouse and taken his identity.

When you first dated and were married, you had an instinct for each other that caused you to do all sorts of beautiful things. You've dropped those things over the years, closing the door on your instincts because you thought you were past that stage. You need not. Those loving, electric touches that were thrilling and exhilarating still have meaning—they still work!

Give yourself a "touch break" once in awhile and trace each other's face. It will get better and better.

Can you look into each other's eyes?   *Your answer:*

Frequently couples say that the best barometer of how their relationship is going is how they're doing with sex. There's no question about it, sex is a good barometer of marriage. However, there are other ways that are even better indicators of a relationship.

One is teasing. When we're really close—when we're experiencing each other fully and meaningfully, the level of teasing is high. There's an affectionate kidding back and forth. It doesn't have a hook or a barb. It is the honest, joyful affection that we share over our special idiosyncrasies. We celebrate our uniqueness with a kind of protective and loving attention.

But the best barometer of all is whether or not we are looking into each other's eyes. When we are appreciating and enjoying each other, we're drawn to look into each other. On some days we may not be. For a quick test to discover where you are in your relationship right now, be still for a few moments and look deeply into your spouse's eyes. The reaction is often a giggle, sometimes a bit of conversation to break the spell, or a shift in our gaze to look elsewhere. If it's a staring contest, try a hug and a kiss and start over.

On the occasions when we're really close, we pour out our true selves through our eyes and draw the other person in. If we're hesitant to look at each other, why? We never had any problem looking into each other's eyes when we were dating. In fact, we didn't want to look any place else. We had that soulful look that people talk about. The fullness of us was not on the tip of our tongues but at the very edge of our eyelids. We were communicating deeply. If we feel we don't need to now because we've communicated that way a lot of times in the past and know each other so well, we're just kidding ourselves.

Looking into each other's eyes is a sign of our closeness, and it is also a means of growing closer.

The main key to a marital relationship is communication. We don't need to search for outside things to bring excitement and satisfaction into our marriage. Our happiness is not dependent on where we live, the amount of money we make, how our children are doing, the places we're able to go for vacations or the friends we have. All those things are important, but at the root of how we're doing in our marriage, is how well we're communicating. Communication in marriage should be something more than the type of communication we have with a relative, a friend or an acquaintance. It isn't just that we have sexual activity. We don't touch other people the way we touch each other. We don't look into someone else's eyes the way we look into our beloved's. The reason is obvious. We're not called to know anybody else with the same depth that we have in a marriage relationship. So we can do better than treat our husbands or wives as acquaintances with moments of sexual intimacy thrown in. The whole aspect of communication is different between a husband and wife. Let's enjoy and appreciate the difference!

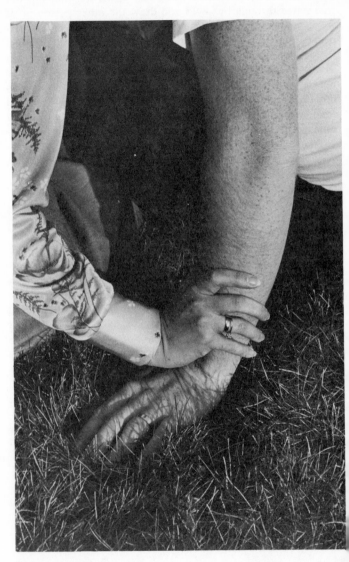

I'm appreciating you.

BETTER THAN TALKING ABOUT
ANYTHING ELSE IS TALKING
ABOUT "US"—MY NEED OF
YOU, YOUR CONCERN FOR
ME, OUR FEARS, OUR HOPES.

4

'COUPLE' TOPICS

What is a good husband?
What is a good wife?

Your answer:

You could have a good discussion or even a debate trying to figure out what a good husband or wife is! Such a topic ought to make good "couple" talk. Everyone has a pretty solid opinion on what the correct answer should be. What's interesting is that every woman has a clear picture of what a good husband is, and every man has firm ideas about the qualities of a good wife. We're sharper-eyed about our mates than we are about ourselves!

Naturally the qualities of a good husband and a good wife will vary, depending on the different sections of the country, ethnic customs and ages. So the Southern ideal of a wife will not be exactly the same as the New York City ideal. A person brought up in a French-oriented family will expect something different in a mate than the one brought up in a Chinese-oriented family. Someone who is 65 will not describe his idea of the perfect spouse in the same way as a person who is 23. The core family of husband, wife and child calls for another set of qualities when it includes aunts, uncles and grandparents. Is this a "couple" topic?

Although modern marriage would call it old-fashioned, we still look for a husband to possess steadiness, reliability and a certain amount of initiative, leadership and strength. We look for a wife to be thoughtful and compassionate, openly showing her enthusiasms and disappointments.

We like to see a husband concerned about providing decent housing and schooling for his family. We expect him to play ball with his sons. We look for him to give advice to his children. We hope he is a handyman, able to fix faucets and washing machines, put up storm windows and make some improvements around the house. We look to him for protection when there's a strange noise in the middle of the night. When there is trouble with one of the neighbors or tradespeople it is the husband who is expected to rectify it. He's expected to be a good neighbor, pleasant, not too involved, but pitching in when necessary. We also look for him to be active in a church or civic organization, from volunteer fireman to Little League coach. He's also expected to excel in whatever job he has, either by going to school, taking part in professional associations, reading periodicals or getting more experience.

We look for the wife to be a good homemaker, able to handle the house and the meals and perhaps a part-time job on the side. She should be more or less child-oriented and up on the latest child-rearing practices. We expect her to be clever at decorating the house and balancing the various needs of the family. We look for the wife to be socially adept, keeping the family popular in the neighborhood and community. We expect her to be an asset to her husband's business. (This must be good "couple" talk.)

We want the husband to be job- and business-oriented. We are tolerant of his losing himself in sports, television, tools or a hobby. He's allowed to have a tenuous ego that his wife has to protect. He is the driver of the car and the complainer about money, the conduct of the children or the activities of his wife, especially in sex. He is supposed to bring excitement into her life and distract her from the dullness of her days.

We are tolerant of a wife's spending a lot of time on the telephone. She's allowed a certain sensitivity that her husband

Let's talk about you and me——"us."

touches at his own risk. We encourage her to be the social director of the family. The children and the house are looked on as being more hers than his.

We could talk on and on, but discussions of the ideal spouse would still be activity-centered and role-oriented and not be "couple" talk. We need to discuss our relationship. That is a "couple" topic. We are to highlight the essence of what it means to be husband and wife, a man and a woman belonging to each other, immersed in and totally alert and responsive to each other. To do otherwise is to miss "us." Once in a rare while we may mention my sensitivity to you or your awareness of me, but if we go on to talk about all sorts of things that we are supposed to do for each other, how we are supposed to act toward our children and the neighbors and on the job and for the world, we turn marriage into a business operation. It is "parenthood," a small-group-for-social-action or a pleasant, compatible roommate situation. Any of them could be handled by a man and a woman whether they were married or not. It might be a convenience if they were married, but marriage is not a necessity.

The basic problem is that after we've been married for a while our notion of marriage changes. When we first dated our whole desire was simply to be together. We wanted to live together, not only physically but with our total beings. We thought of marriage with great expectations. We would have the opportunity to be completely involved with each other, spending all our time together.

The years have passed and now we have lost that single-mindedness. We say to ourselves, "Well, we really deluded ourselves about being married. It's not possible to live the way we imagined. Life goes on and it is serious. We have all sorts of responsibilities and we can't spend a lot of time with each other. We have to do important and significant things. We have our children to take care of, our bills to pay and a world to change."

But the point of being husband and wife is to have a "couple" relationship. We started out with it. What happened to it? Oh, we still care for each other and the other person is the most important one in our lives. We want to talk things over together, but not so much to enjoy our oneness as to get co-operation or support for wherever our attention is centered.

When you see the word "husband" on a page, you automatically think "marriage" and "wife." The same thing is true of the word "wife"—you obviously think of "marriage" and "husband." Our wifeliness or our husbandliness should be the core of who we are, not our job or our dream for this world or for our children. "Wife" or "husband" is part of our identity. As we live our lives out, our marriage should be "us." It shouldn't be something that we do—an activity in which we're engaged. For no matter how essential or important we consider it to be, it's not the purpose for our becoming a couple. We are to appreciate the "us" of marriage. We are to be the focus of our concentration in life.

We tend to look on being a husband or wife as a responsibility we have assumed. We realize that we have to consider this other person in the decisions we're making for the present or in our plans for the future. But our marriage isn't our whole life. There are many other facets that make up our life. Many things assume a greater importance than our marriage. We fit marriage into our life, instead of fitting our life into our marriage. In fact, we look on the latter idea as sort of selfish; we think there are bigger ambitions in life than marriage. We don't want to be tied down to a marriage situation. We see ourselves as having more talent than that, greater breadth of vision, a bigger contribution to make to the world. We look on marriage as stifling.

But wait a minute. No greater contribution could be made for the well-being and stability of this world than for every couple to engage in a full marriage. We could spend our time trying to find meaning and fulfillment by being "significant." We could also occupy ourselves in good activities and still have nothing but a hollow heart and a desperate longing for something more. On the other hand, a person who engages in a full marriage is fulfilled—wondrously.

A full marriage can't be an extracurricular activity, a sideline. It can't be something that's nice to have but which

121

Our children are great, Honey, but you are my delight.

doesn't absorb the fullness of who we are. The most cosmic experience we can have is to engage in a true love affair with each other. Nothing could be a greater ambition than that.

It's because of false notions and propaganda that people do so poorly in their marriages. A husband and wife don't need to meet every outside demand. They should pool their full talents and capabilities *in the service of their relationship with each other.* When they do, their marriage will not be getting the leftovers, it will be first rate!

Part of the reason for a couple's not giving their relationship pre-eminence is that they're afraid. "What if the other lets me down?" each asks. "What if he doesn't respond in the way I need?" So, to protect themselves, they have all sorts of escape hatches and safety valves on which to rely. A career, a hobby, the children. And they find it a lot easier to do nice things for each other once in a while than to have a full-fledged marriage relationship.

Furthermore, with all their activities they have plenty to talk about. They don't even realize they have other things—more meaningful things—to discuss.

This is a perfect example of having something right under our nose and missing it. *Our real calling in life is to each other!* It is from that point that we go on to our children, families, neighbors and the world. Our true fulfillment in life is not to bring the world into our relationship, but to take our relationship into the world! It's not to have a passion for mankind, but to be devoted to each other! It's not to raise children, it's to delight in each other! It's not to provide security for my spouse; it's to provide *myself* for my spouse! It's not to live side by side over the years doing all the right things that are expected of a husband or a wife, but to be absorbed in each other!

What is the most important topic for you and your beloved to discuss?

Your answer:

The most important thing for businessmen to talk about is business. The most important thing for doctors to talk about is medicine. So what would we expect mothers—as mothers—to talk about? Their children, of course. Then it should be understood that the natural topic and most important aspect of a husband and wife's communication is their married relationship—their coupleness.

Talking about *us*—our interaction, what we mean to each other, how we respond, listen and are aware of each other—is the most important topic for our conversations. Of course we will also need to talk about the activities of the day, family obligations, feelings about the boss, the children's needs and our accomplishments, but the most meaningful conversation is where I stand with you, how you see me, how I'm feeling about you and what can help me understand you better. Something good happens to us as we live and grow together.

One of the most significant commitments in marriage is that we are to communicate with each other in the most intimate, deepest and total way possible. We are to completely reveal ourselves physically, mentally, psychologically and spiritually, and we are to be totally open to listening to that revelation of the other person. By not communicating, a man can do all the "right" things and still not be a good husband, and a woman can exhaust herself in living up to her responsibilities and still not be a good wife. But if they are constantly "in touch," communicating with each other in the fullest and deepest sense of that term, they fulfill one of the most significant commitments of being a husband or a wife.

What do you talk about?   *Your answer:*

The children, our work, the relatives and the night's television programs are likely subjects of conversations, and in all probability we talk about the thing that happens to be uppermost in our mind at any given moment. We don't plan out our conversations, we just talk at random, the choice of topic pretty well determined by what hangs heaviest over each of us.

I choose a topic according to its impact on *me*. It may bother me or attract me, but it is pertinent to *me*. This is a non-married way to go about things. It's self-centered. I may think I'm bringing it up because I want your input, your advice or direction, or (and this is more likely) I want you to

Exploring our deepest feelings about tragedy develops our "oneness."

do something for me or to change the way you're acting. You do the same. Still, with all that, the fundamental urgency behind our choice of topics comes from our self-interest. So we are two people, each pushing his own personal desire.

Sometimes the topic is chosen just to fill the silence with conversation. We talk about the headlines in the paper, the weather, who has done what where. Or we express a disjointed series of unrelated thoughts that pop into our minds.

At times our conversation can be considered entertainment, intended to keep the other person interested. This is why our topics cover business, budget, taxes, discipline, social reports about our mutual families, neighborhood gossip, vacations, the house, retirement, decisions that have to be made—anything and everything.

In any marriage, in even the quietest one, there has been a volume of words poured out on each other over the years. A relatively small percentage of those words concern our coupleness. We talk as companions. We don't talk as husbands and wives. It's time we developed a new perspective—one focused in on us!

Doris had always hated to talk about death, much less experience it in any degree of closeness. So whenever she and her husband Tom attended a wake, he tried to keep the conversation light and on safe topics. He figured that a good night's sleep would calm things down and she would get over it.

After the death of a neighbor, Doris decided to face her fear. Over a cup of coffee before going to bed, Doris said, "Look, Tom, the same thing happens every time death comes around. We tiptoe around it. I don't like to talk about it because I'm upset, and you try to get me distracted. But you don't know why I'm upset or what's going on inside me. And I have no idea at all what you feel when it comes to death. We've got to talk about it. I don't want you to make me feel better. I don't want you to give me an answer. I don't want you to treat me as a problem. I just want you to listen and try to experience a little of what I'm experiencing. Then I want you to tell me what's going on inside you."

Tom wasn't too sure it was a good idea. He knew how churned up she got, but Doris meant business.

"We say we know everything about each other and that we understand each other so well. But about death you don't know me at all, because I haven't let you. What gets to me about death is that I see your name in every death notice I read. I see you in the casket at every wake we go to. I envision the years of loneliness without you. I don't want to live without you. You mean everything to me, and I'm convinced in my heart that you're going to die before I do. I can't stand the thought of not hearing your step on the front step anymore, of the chair opposite me being vacant. And how can I ever sleep without you beside me? My life is so entwined with yours, how could I ever call it life without you?"

Tom was stunned. He had always figured he would be the first to go, and he was quite content for it to happen that way. But he hadn't put himself in Doris' shoes. Now he did, and he felt some of the black aloneness that terrified her. He shuddered. Doris felt his shudder and knew that he was feeling her feelings. They held each other tightly. It was a real moment of understanding for both of them. "You have loved me in many ways," Tom said, "but I've never felt more of your love than I do at this moment."

I've been wanting to learn more about God. How do you feel about Him?

Do you talk much about you two?   *Your answer:*

Most people talk about themselves. I talk about myself; you talk about yourself; but we don't talk much about "us." It's probably because we've let our interests develop elsewhere. Our goals in life don't center around us as much as we may think. We can see where our prime attention is by what we choose to talk about. We may think that our choice of conversation is accidental, but it comes out of a pattern of thought. A boy who talks about sports all the time is sports-minded. A girl who is always talking about boys is considered boy-crazy.

We think somebody at a party is a bore because he is a Johnny-One-Note. All he can talk about is the one topic that is the overriding concern in his life. Of course if we're interested in that topic, then he's a scintillating conversationalist!

So what do we talk about? By looking at our conversations and noticing the frequency of a topic or a pattern of issues we can discover where our real interests lie. A man can say he's not job-oriented. He may mean that he's not striving to get ahead. But he's always talking about the job—how much he dislikes it and how bad it is. He's actually just as job-oriented as the one who's very positive about his work.

The same thing is true about a woman. She may believe that she's not like her mother used to be, all wrapped up in her children. But her topic of conversation may revolve around the children as much as her mother's did. She may complain about them, say she's hedged in and doesn't have the freedom to get ahead the way she wants to, but she's just as child-oriented as the one who is content with her children.

The basic reason why we choose our children or something else outside ourselves for the dominant portion of our conversation is because we don't have to get deeply involved. Of course we're close to our children, but we're in charge of them, so we're in a king-servant position no matter how democratic we may appear to be. With our job, although we may be dependent upon it and involved, we are outside it.

Because we do love each other and don't want to live separate lives, we need to put *us* into our discussions, and get some practice! There's a lot of involvement ahead. It will take courage to talk often about *us*. But it's right and good— and worth it!

Why shouldn't you talk about you two?   *Your answer:*

When we are absorbed in our husband-and-wife relationship, we can't help talking about it, and we learn more and more about each other as we talk. We are conscious of the various nuances of our relationship. We are sensitive to what is going on inside us. When we don't give much conversation to our couple relationship, we are not much more than companions, partners or pleasant acquaintances. The less we talk about *us,* the less involved we are with each other.

We may be brilliant conversationalists, but when we're not talking about us and are talking about other areas, we are developing our sensitivities in connection with them. We throw our talents into developing our capabilities and our responsiveness to whatever is the main focus of our life. If the focus is *us,* we experience full closeness; if not, something else has our attention and we are less close.

Grace and Thomas recognized that their children were their main focus. They realized that their coupleness should be of first importance, so they decided not to talk about the children unless it was necessary. They did not exclude every reference to them but made being husband and wife dominant in their conversations. As the days went by, Grace and Thomas saw a change in their awareness of each other and experienced a greater degree of closeness than they had ever experienced before. They began to develop their real capabilities as husband and wife. They began to achieve their potential greatness as lovers.

When our interests are outside of our couple relationship we have dull days and much grayness in our marriage. Chores get to us and we wonder whether or not it's all worthwhile. "What am I getting out of this?" we start asking ourselves.

But self-centeredness and selfishness is the result when each of us talks about his own topics. However, because we're good, decent people, we'll try to give each other equal time, and we appreciate any degree of similarity of interests. Take note: there is one topic of conversation in which each of us can be equally involved and each has a total stake—*us!* We can experience the same intensity of interest, the same solid absorption. When we're engrossed in each other, the skies are sunny.

Marion couldn't find words for her feelings until she heard the song, "Is That All There Is?" Peggy Lee sang about emptiness and that's just where Marion and Ken were. Timidly Marion brought up the subject of their marriage. "Well, when I come home," said Ken, "we get the business of our marriage straightened out. I check the mail, find out about the children, talk about any social obligations we have. I let you know what went on at the office. We might talk about plans for a vacation or a new car." He took a deep breath. "We're old married people—dull, dull, dull." Marion nodded her head. "We could pose for the typical married couple. Even when we go out for an evening we never really get away. We are never 'us.' We just talk about things in our lives."

The next day they called a baby sitter and that evening they went out—without the children—for the purpose of getting beyond the "things."

It was a strange meal. They found they had built up such

habits of talking about everything except each other that there were awkward silences. It amazed them how little they could find to say without the crutches of the children, the house, the job. When they were dating and first married they couldn't stop talking to each other about each other. They'd be at the beach all day long, but after he'd taken her home, he'd still have to call her, and they'd still go on and on over the phone.

With a final cup of coffee, Marion almost gave up, but then Ken mentioned how he thought about life after five years of being married. They talked about how much and how little difference the years had made in the way each of them felt about life. Wow! They had a lot of catching up to do!

Art was an accountant with a large firm in New Jersey. One morning driving in to work he was nervous. In his pocket was a note from his boss. All it said was, "See me as soon as you get in tomorrow."

Art went directly to his boss' office. Mr. Knutson wasted no time. "I always believe in letting my employees know where they stand with me. I'm giving you a $50 a week raise because you've got your head screwed on right. A lot of guys just put in their time, but your heart is with the company. Sometimes wives mess things up, demanding too much attention. Either you have a sensible wife or you've got her under control. Of course, the further you get ahead the better it's going to be for her in the long run. Keep up the good work and there's no telling how far you can go."

Art couldn't wait to get to the phone to tell Phyllis about the $50 a week. There was so much they needed. The old washing machine would be the first thing to go. Then they could get a new rug and not keep tripping over the old one. They could get a second car so she wouldn't be stranded all day. There were so many things!

His mind was in a whirl as he told Phyllis about it. She said she was pleased, but there was an edge in her voice that Art didn't recognize. He started to look at the life Phyllis had. All she ever heard him talk about was getting ahead. Of course, both of them understood he was doing it for her and

Another romantic evening with you.

A toast to you and me . . . tonight . . . alone . . . together.

the children. But he started to wonder if it was worth it. "In the long run" were the words his boss used. Art had used them himself when planning out their life, but now he wondered what kind of a "long run" it would be if it sacrificed all the present. When I do get to the top, what will we talk about then? I'm treating Phyllis the same way the boss is treating me. He rewards me as long as I go along with his line of thinking. I'm very generous with Phyllis, but I'm making her live my way. He wanted to talk the whole thing over with her. He found his palms sweating. He couldn't believe he was getting so nervous. They'd been married for seven years and had always gotten along well. But he wasn't sure what her reaction would be. Maybe she liked everything the way it was and didn't want to change. He helped her with the dishes and with bathing the children so they could sit down to talk sooner. When finally they were alone, he found himself tongue-tied.

"Phyllis," he started several times.

"Art, what's the matter? Did something awful happen at work? I've never seen you like this."

"No, it's not the job, Phyllis, and yet, I guess it is. I guess I want to be more than just a successful businessman. Most especially, I want to mean more to you. I'm beginning to see the job as dominating us. The boss said I must have you under control. His words were to the effect that we were concentrating on the future as he and his wife were. What bothers me most is that from externals he has every right to expect that I would be just like him, not caring much about now. But as I think about it, I don't want to be like him— and I don't want us to be like them.

"Help me to stop talking about the job. I don't want to be important because of what I can provide for you. I want to be important to you as *me, now*."

A tear ran down Phyllis's cheek, "I just don't believe this. I had given up hope. With this raise, I was thinking I had lost you for good—that I would have to resign myself to just climbing up the ladder with you. But I love you so much when you're just you and not the businessman. Yes, let's take time to be us. I know the job is part of your life and I enjoy sharing it with you, but you're so much more—and I want all of you."

What could change your pattern of conversation?

Your answer:

Our pattern of conversation is developed over the years, undulating with the changes in our life. In school we were probably concerned with assignments or activities or dating. As a married couple, we are apt to be concentrating on the children or household duties or a job and on paying the bills. Our beloved will, in some cases, be more aware of what we talk about than we are, and we'll be more aware of what he brings up—because we're conscious of each other's subjects. We will be defensive about what we talk about. We will want to excuse ourselves. We will want to explain away and justify why we talk so much about a certain topic. But let's be honest and openly recognize just how much we've been talking about everything else—and not *us*. Couple conversation doesn't include us as doers, providers, as parents, as neighbors or churchgoers. It centers on *us* in relationship to each other—"husband" (not just a man who happens to be married) and "wife" (not just a woman who has a wedding ring).

Recognition of the problem area starts the process of change. Then we can face up to whether or not we want to be married. The question is not whether we want to be married to each other, the question is whether we want to be married at all. Maybe we don't want to be married; maybe we just

Last night we discovered a whole new world. Tonight, and tomorrow night, too, I want to tell you why I love you so much.

want to live together with benefit of clergy. However, if we want to be "one" in the true sense of marriage, we really need to make our relationship more important to us than anything else on earth. These are more than pretty words. They are more than a love-story saying. They express the reality to which marriage calls us. Walking down the aisle doesn't automatically give us the desire to make our relationship top priority. For instance, a woman can have a baby without having a particularly strong desire to bring up that child. It can be little more than a physical event. She may even rear the child out of a sense of duty and not have any real heart for it. A man may take a certain job and perform competently without having wanted the job or being trained for it. He does it because it gives him good money or because it's the only job he can get.

If we want to make being a husband and wife something more than a romantic accident or a sideline activity, we have to make an honest decision to recognize *us* above everything else. We can't make only a pious wish or a New Year's resolution. It has to be a genuine commitment to begin to live that way. The decision is the key thing. We choose to marry. We can choose to live out that relationship on a daily basis.

For instance, a usual subject of conversation between a husband and wife is their work. When the husband comes in the door, the wife asks, "How was your day?" Both of them interpret that question to mean, "Tell me what you did; let me know some of the exciting things that happened, pass on some of the news." But, "How was your day?" should be, "Tell me about *you,* what went on within you and what happened to you as a person during the course of your day."

Feelings, values and dreams play a very large role in any conversation that concerns you and me—the "us-ness" of our relationship.

The listening aspect in an "us" conversation is concentrated more on appreciation and understanding than on coming up with an answer or plan.

The deciding is the necessary first step, but then it takes awareness and practice. We need to be aware of when we get off the main topic—which is *us*—and move back onto it. Of course other things have to be talked about, but they can be talked about briefly, never being allowed to monopolize our conversations. Our interaction as husband-and-wife is to be dominant.

What excuses do you use for not talking about yourselves?

Your answer:

The logical excuse used by almost everybody for not doing certain things nowadays is not having enough time. We spend little time even with those we love a great deal. We have many obligations and responsibilities calling for discussion. We want to talk about us when we get a chance, but the chances seldom come. We feel caught, so we figure that tomorrow we'll have time for each other. But tomorrow never comes.

The children are a legitimate excuse, too. They're only going to be around for a certain length of time. The kids are a big conversation consumer, but we feel we don't have any choice, that we have to sacrifice what we'd rather talk about in order to live up to our responsibility toward them. After the kids leave home, we'll talk about us.

That far-off goal is a dream, because if we haven't been talking much about us for 20 or 30 years, we won't be able to suddenly do it when the kids are gone. We can't instantly change the long-time pattern. What's likely to happen is that instead of talking about the kids, we'll talk about the grand-kids!

The job takes our attention the same way the children do. Richard says, "Well, right now I am concentrating on my job because this is the time when I have to get ahead. After a while I'll settle into a niche, and I can do my work without thinking so much about it. Then I'll be able to give more time and attention to Jan—and *us*." But it doesn't work that way! Later on Richard will be thinking about his retirement plan and pension and how to get a little more on that, how to make provisions for the time when they don't have a regular paycheck.

Richard and Jan also feel that the house has to be taken care of. They think that once they get the house straightened out they'll have more time together, appreciating each other. But they never will get the house the way they want it, because as soon as they finish one thing, something else will take up their attention—and their conversation. People can continually upgrade their homes, and then they have to redo everything because what they did in the first place has worn out.

The amazing thing about most excuses is that they're completely real—and completely irrelevant! As important as are the job, the house, the children, they aren't always the most pressing issues. *We* are—or should be—the most pressing issue even if we don't have any particular problem. We don't have to abdicate every day!

We had better realize that if *we* never get first on our agenda, we don't really want to be important to each other. Not talking about *us* for a couple of days could happen accidentally, but when it turns out that way almost every day, we have to look for the reason. It could be that we're more interested in what's going on in relationships other than our own.

Because we have a limited amount of time together as husband and wife, we can choose to spend that time talking about what we consider most important. We can decide that "we" will take a lion's share of time available to us. It may be that on some days we won't have a great deal of time, but we can take a part of whatever is available. Then we won't lose out entirely!

Because our time usually does come in snippets it is a problem. We have five minutes before supper or ten minutes afterwards or a few minutes when we're driving somewhere. It's difficult to get into anything serious or complicated because there's not enough time to finish it. There have been occasions when we felt there wasn't time to open up and talk about each other, so we chit-chatted about inconsequential things. Yes, it would be nice if we had a string of hours and perfect circumstances, when the kids were quiet and nobody else was around. But if we really want to talk about something, we will make time for it, no matter what. Let's make ourselves top priority, now!

What practical steps could you take to talk more about you two?   *Your answer:*

We've had a good life, but we've got a lot of catching up to do. It's not too late to talk about us!

When a husband comes home from work, the first thing he starts talking about is what he's been thinking about in the car, on the train or walking to the door. If his job, the kids, the lawn, taxes or the mail are in the forefront of his consciousness, that's what he'll begin to talk about. He won't suddenly talk to his wife about their relationship if that hasn't been on his mind.

A wife can be almost taken by surprise when her husband arrives, even though she knows he comes home on the 5:32 and walks up the steps at the same time every day. Her concern is that supper be ready, and she's got to tell him the washing machine has broken down, or what Aunt Tessie said when she called.

There's nothing bad about the situation in itself. But it's a wasted opportunity. In these moments a relationship can be advanced—if we think about it beforehand. We wouldn't think about getting a car, switching jobs or buying a house without a great deal of thought. When we go to a real estate agent, we've concentrated on what we're looking for so that we don't talk off the top of our heads. We'd feel foolish if we did that. Yet that's the way we act with each other. We just say whatever is on the tip of our tongues. It often takes a jolt to wake us up, to get us into bringing out our feelings on the major things of life.

Beth, a friend from years ago, wrote me about what happened when her husband's mother died. Her death had been sudden and at that moment Vic turned to ice. Afterwards, on the way home, Beth wanted to talk but she didn't know what to say. Her heart went out to Vic. She wanted to say something, anything that would take the rigid look off his face. She knew he was holding himself back, trying to be strong.

They finally pulled into the driveway. She was glad they were home. It had been a strange and difficult ride. The 15 minutes had seemed like hours. In the house Vic went immediately to their room, and she, as gently as she could, broke the news to the children that Grandma was in heaven. Once she had settled the children for the night, she thought Vic might appreciate a cup of coffee. She busied herself preparing it. He still didn't appear so she went into their bedroom. She found him sitting on the bed, sobbing his heart out. At first she couldn't believe her eyes. She had never seen Vic cry before. She just didn't know what to do. She went over and sat down beside him and held his hand. Then it all poured out of him. "I feel so powerless. I want to yell, I want to kick in walls. I want to plead and beg for just a few more years for Mom. I feel there's a part of me gone now. I feel guilty too. A lot of times I wasn't very thoughtful of her. I wish I had called her more often. I'm sorry we didn't have her see more of the children. She always sent special cookies. The kids called them Grandma Cookies . . . and I hate myself for not being a man about all this. I don't like being so weak."

Beth felt her love expanding, enveloping him. She had never felt closer to him. She held his hand against her face and kissed the palm. She leaned her head on his shoulder and put her arms around him and held him tight.

The whole time of the wake and funeral was very precious for both of them. They talked more often, in greater depth and more personally than they had in years. Vic talked about his fears of dying before he could provide adequately for her and the children. Beth spoke of her constant concern to prepare the children for a full life. They listened to each other and understood and loved each other.

When we get up in the morning we think about what our day involves. We know what work lies ahead at the office, what we have to do for the kids—take them to the dentist or to dancing classes or to a ballfield—what cleaning or cooking has to be done. As we get those things under control we think about our plans for the evening. Maybe it's going to be a pleasant night just watching television. Maybe we will visit an old friend. As we plan, we have a rough idea of when we're going to be together, but when we are, we tend to look over each other's heads. The other person is there, as a shadow figure in the background, but our eyes are zeroed in on other events and persons. Any time we treat other people or our children that way, we don't do very well with them.

The same is true of a husband-and-wife relationship. The amount of thought we put into it indicates the value we place on it. When we care about what we're going to tell the other person, we can think in terms of how it will affect our rela-

Life with you is so beautiful. I can't bear the thought of one of us dying.

tionship. I can go beyond my thinking that you're going to be pleased to know of a promotion or that you're going to be delighted with the letter we received from your brother. The promotion means we can pay a baby sitter and go out to dinner—just us. And hearing from your brother means everything is all right and we, together, can appreciate him again.

We can think through how we will talk about listening better to each other, or how to be more open and honest about what's going on inside us. We can consider as a topic of conversation the ways in which we can be more sensitive to each other. These are the things we have to learn to talk about.

We need to set aside specific times for us. If we don't, it won't happen. Our days will shoot by us and we won't know where they've gone. There are so many things competing for our attention that if we don't give ourselves a specific time every day, we'll miss out having any time at all.

I know a couple who realized the situation. Ben's mother had a stroke, and while she was still in the hospital he and Fran realized something had to be done. Her speech was returning and the doctors were very reassuring about her being able to walk again, but she could no longer live by herself.

They decided she should live with them.

"Okay," Ben said, "let's make some plans. For us. What with the office, the kids, the house—and Mom—it's going to be hard to make sure we even have time to talk."

"That's it," said Fran. "How about half an hour after the supper dishes. But let's not talk about the kids or leaky faucets, the bills or the office. Let's concentrate on what you and I have been feeling."

Ben and Fran made it a practice and within six months after his mother had moved in with them, they both felt that it had been the best thing that had ever happened to them. "I can't say I always enjoy having her around," Ben confided to Fran. "She gets cranky with the kids and tries to boss me, but having a half hour with you all to myself makes everything all right."

All of us can find a half hour for something important. There may be extraordinary days when that time doesn't come about, but in the normal pattern of our lives, we will have 30 minutes that we can spend with each other—especially as we find out how much we delight in it! That time is for us, not to catch up on the events of the day or to fritter away with chit-chat, but to concentrate on building up our consciousness, our awareness, our responsiveness to each other. We want to sharpen the ability that we have been given to build our love relationship.

We can train the children to give us that time. We spend a good number of hours with them, and we can explain that we have time with them and time with each other. It's important for them to recognize that there's a relationship in the house other than parenthood! The whole reason for their being is *us*. Therefore, they have a stake in our being the most *us* we can possibly be. Children will actually encourage us to have this time. They'll become protective of it. They'll call us down if we miss it, because they'll have noticed what happens when we don't take our time for *us*. They'll notice we're less understanding of them, less patient, less tolerant and more demanding.

To make those minutes for us, sacrifices may have to be made—to take the phone off the hook or to forget our favorite television show. But the rewards are great.

Some husbands and wives seem to be forever in love. A couple I know were out celebrating their twelfth anniversary when they were interrupted by another couple. The woman was matronly with a kindly face and the man was tall and distinguished looking. They offered Dan and Nancy their congratulations and best wishes. Startled, Dan asked how they knew they were celebrating their anniversary.

"Anniversary?" the gentleman said. "You're on your honeymoon, aren't you?"

Nancy started to giggle and Dan looked very pleased. "We better not be honeymooners. We have an 11-year-old daughter."

"Well, isn't that marvelous," the woman said. "You look so much in love."

"We are!" they proclaimed together.

After the couple had left Nancy beamed. "We must be doing something right."

145

This picnic is just for us.

"It all started here on our last anniversary. Remember, Nancy? We decided to take some time every day for us to talk, to put everything else aside and make us number one for a little while."

"And look what it did for us! We've had the best year of all. We get better 'by the dozen.' "

"I've never loved you more," said Dan.

"Our fights are fewer and shorter," said Nancy.

"And I look forward to getting home everyday as soon as I can."

"And you keep surprising me with little presents and cards. I feel like a teenager again."

"I never realized how much fun it would be to keep on doing silly, romantic things with you. I love you, sweetheart."

To make the time count, whether it's five minutes or an hour, we can decide ahead of time what facet of our relationship we're going to discuss that evening. If we don't, each of us will come to our talking time with his own topic and the other will be unprepared. Our phone calls during the day are often just check-in jobs—I remind you to pick up the milk and you wonder if there is any special mail today; we make a few comments about the weather or the traffic or something that came over the news. Instead, I can let you know I'm thinking about *us* and we can settle on what we want to talk about together.

Some people feel that this is a bit much. Why should a couple go that heavily into their talking together—even to programming the time? The simple answer is that it doesn't work any other way. We expect to program time for our children. Let's do it for ourselves, too!

Why should you plan for your conversations with each other?   *Your answer:*

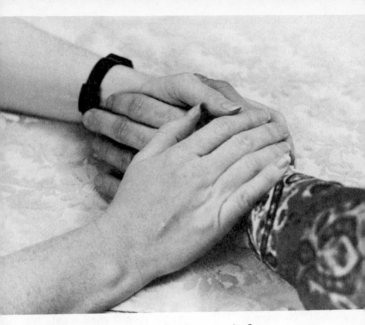

Some couples seem to be forever in love.

First and foremost, planning for our conversations makes each of us loom larger on the other's horizon. During the day, even when we're not in each other's presence, our living reflects our relationship.

The memory of the previous night's conversation lingers. We think about each other more frequently during the day. The fact that we know we're going to be talking together that half hour in the evening reminds us of each other during the day. It gives us something to look forward to.

Furthermore, conversations lead to more conversations. The more we talk together about each other the more we have to talk about.

When old friends meet they often find they don't have much in common any more. They were very dear friends and no barrier has been intentionally raised between them—but their bonds are not recent. Much has happened to each of them that didn't involve the other. The same is true of a husband-and-wife relationship. When their activities have been separate for any length of time, each has changed, minutely or greatly. They find themselves reaching for conversation or filling the air with a lot of chatter. The more often they are together and the more aware they are of each other, the more they interest each other and the more they understand, appreciate and love each other.

In other words, we become experts on each other, picking up every nuance, alert to every new bit of information, able to piece together little scraps of evidence, finding each other tremendously significant.

Many of our problems will disappear. The more I know you and you know me and the more I get absorbed in you and you get absorbed in me, the more the petty details and niggling frustrations will diminish. We'll have a refreshing, life-giving perspective.

Al and Vivian found that to be true. They had miserable fights at first. They recognized that their fights were not good ones. They didn't finish them and clear the air. And one night it was particularly bad. After the flare-up there was dead silence. Both of them stayed seated. It was almost as if to leave was a surrender. Both studiously avoided catching

149

the other person's eye. Al had a firm grip on his paper. Vivian was absorbed in her book. The television program went on and on in the background.

Finally Al threw down his paper, turned off the TV and said, "Look, Vivian, by all normal standards, we're supposed to be bright people. But we're really dumb."

"Oh, you want to fight some more?"

"No, that's exactly it. I don't want to fight any more. But we're doing so much that it really comes down to just one big, long fight. You tell me that I never talk to you, and I ask you what there is to talk about. You're upset because I don't say anything and I get all hot and bothered because you're always asking me questions about what went on in the office and giving me all the details of every little runny nose and scraped knee. What's the matter with us? I don't remember your being this way when we first got married. And I don't remember being 'Silent Sam.' I know it's not good not to talk, but I honestly can't think of anything to say. I'm really not trying to bug you. I just can't think of anything. I know I should take more interest in what the kids are doing and the little things that happen to them. But we can't talk about that all night. Besides, sometimes when you start talking about Jimmy falling off the bike or Mary having a fever, I'm worried about what's going on at the office. It involves a lot, and I don't know whether or not I'm up to it, or, maybe I have a meeting with the boss the next day and I'm afraid of what he's going to say."

There was a stunned look on Vivian's face. She had started out of her chair but now she leaned back as if the strength had gone out of her legs. "You worried?" she asked in a very low tone of voice. There was a gentleness about her that reminded him of the girl that he had married. He hadn't seen that in her in a long time. "Oh, Al, I'm so glad. I don't mean that I enjoy your being worried. But I'm so happy that you're not the rock that I thought you had become. Don't you see, dear? I have to know what's going on inside you. Otherwise I'm going to jump to all sorts of conclusions. You're right about all the questions that I ask and the little things that I talk about not being important. But we are. I'll forget all the silly little stuff. Let's talk about how we feel. Whether we're happy or glad or upset or worried or eager or gloomy or whatever it is. I really do want to know you—and I want you to know what I'm like."

Since that night when Al and Vivian started to talk their life improved. Al still had a hard time finding his feelings because he'd done such a good job of pretending that he didn't have any, but he was getting more and more comfortable. He appreciated Vivian's patience and realized how much she helped him. After a particularly lengthy description of his feelings one evening, Al gave her a hug. "Now I bet you're sorry, because when I get going I really get going!"

"Oh, Al, that's when it's best of all."

Yes, the misunderstandings between us because we don't talk enough will simply disappear. Fights will become fewer and shorter. And gentleness and understanding will increase day by day. Our marriage will become more and more dominant in our consciousness. Everything else will fit into the context of our marriage rather than our marriage having to beg for attention in our lives.

We will use the moments of time—even the smallest ones —to advantage. We'll be able to talk together more meaningfully at any time.

Our success will be determined by how well we do with each other rather than by any other norm. Our life will be in the hands of our beloved—the one who loves us more than anybody else on the face of this earth.

In later life there won't be so many moments of regret asking "Why didn't I tell her this?" or, "Did he know how much I loved him?" Those questions are often asked when it's too late!

But today is not too late. Our best years lie ahead. We will not ask "What am I getting out of life?" Instead we will exclaim, "How can life be so full!" and realize we've only just begun.

OTHER IMAGE BOOKS

OTHER IMAGE BOOKS

OTHER IMAGE BOOKS

OTHER IMAGE BOOKS

OTHER IMAGE BOOKS

THE PERFECT JOY OF ST. FRANCIS – Felix Timmermans. Trans. by Raphael Brown

THE POWER AND THE WISDOM – John L. McKenzie

THE POWER OF LOVE – Fulton J. Sheen

POWER TO THE PARENTS! – Joseph and Lois Bird

THE PRACTICE OF THE PRESENCE OF GOD – Trans. with an Intro. by John J. Delaney

THE PSALMS OF THE JERUSALEM BIBLE – Alexander Jones, General Editor

RELIGION AND WORLD HISTORY – Christopher Dawson. Ed. by James Oliver and Christina Scott

A RELIGIOUS HISTORY OF THE AMERICAN PEOPLE (2 vols.) – Sydney E. Ahlstrom

RENEWING THE EARTH – Ed. by David J. O'Brien and Thomas A. Shannon

REVELATIONS OF DIVINE LOVE – Trans. with an Intro. by M. L. del Mastro

THE ROMAN CATHOLIC CHURCH – John L. McKenzie

THE RULE OF ST. BENEDICT – Trans. and ed., with an Intro., by Anthony C. Meisel and M. L. del Mastro

ST. FRANCIS OF ASSISI – G. K. Chesterton

ST. FRANCIS OF ASSISI – Johannes Jorgensen

SAINT THOMAS AQUINAS – G. K. Chesterton

SAINTS FOR ALL SEASONS – John J. Delaney, editor

A SENSE OF LIFE, A SENSE OF SIN – Eugene Kennedy

THE SEXUAL CELIBATE – Donald Goergen

SHOULD ANYONE SAY FOREVER? – John C. Haughey

THE SHROUD OF TURIN (Revised Edition) – Ian Wilson

THE SIGN OF JONAS – Thomas Merton

THE SINAI MYTH – Andrew M. Greeley

SOMETHING BEAUTIFUL FOR GOD – Malcolm Muggeridge

THE SOUL AFIRE: REVELATIONS OF THE MYSTICS – Ed. by H. A. Reinhold

THE SPIRIT OF CATHOLICISM – Karl Adam

SPIRITUAL CANTICLE – St. John of the Cross. Trans. and ed., with an Intro., by E. Allison Peers

THE SPIRITUAL EXERCISES OF ST. IGNATIUS – Trans. by Anthony Mottola, Ph.D. Intro. by Robert W. Gleason, S.J.

THE STAIRWAY OF PERFECTION – Trans. and ed. by M. L. del Mastro

STORM OF GLORY – John Beevers

OTHER IMAGE BOOKS

A 80 – 6